Gaslighting

How to recognise manipulative
and emotionally abusive people
...and break freee

DR STEPHANIE MOULTON SARKIS

First published in the United States in 2018 by Da Capo Press
an imprint of Perseus Books, LLC, a subsidiary of Hachette Book Group, Inc.
1290 Avenue of the Americas, New York, NY 10104

This edition published in Great Britain in 2019 by Orion Spring
an imprint of The Orion Publishing Group Ltd
Carmelite House, 50 Victoria Embankment
London EC4Y 0DZ

An Hachette UK Company

1 3 5 7 9 10 8 6 4 2

Every effort has been made to ensure that the information in the book is accurate.
The information in this book may not be applicable in each individual case so it is advised
that professional medical advice is obtained for specific health matters and before changing
any medication or dosage. Neither the publisher nor author accepts any legal responsibility
for any personal injury or other damage or loss arising from the use of the information in
this book. In addition, if you are concerned about your diet or exercise regime and
wish to change them, you should consult a health practitioner first.

Print book interior design by Linda Mark
A CIP catalogue record for this book is available from the British Library.
ISBN (Trade paperback) 978 1 4091 8787 5
ISBN (eBook) 978 1 4091 8788 2
Printed in Great Britain by CPI Group (UK) Ltd,
Croydon, CR0 4YY

MIX
Paper from
responsible sources
FSC® C104740

www.orionbooks.co.uk

ORION
SPRING

To everyone who is experiencing gaslighting—
may you find light, hope, and healing.

CONTENTS

INTRODUCTION

YOU KNOW THE GASLIGHTER. HE'S THE CHARMER—THE WITTY, CON-
fident, but overly controlling date. She's the woman on your team
who always manages to take credit for your good work. He's the neighbor who swears you've been putting your garbage into his trash cans,
the politician who can never admit to a mistake, the harasser who says
you asked for it. Gaslighters are master controllers and manipulators, often challenging your very sense of reality. And they can be found everywhere. International political figures, celebrities, your boss, your sibling
or parent, a friend, your coworker, your neighbor, your partner—any
one of these people is in a position to gaslight.

Gaslighters will convince us that we are crazy, that we are abusive,
that we are a huge bundle of problems and no one else will want us, that
we are terrible employees who haven't been fired yet just by the grace of

God, that we are terrible parents who shouldn't have had children, that we have no idea how to manage our own life, or that we are a burden to others. They are toxic.

With the 2016 presidential election and all the noise about "alternative facts" and "fake news," the term *gaslighting* has seen a surge in popularity. (If our confidence in our trusted news sources can be shaken fully enough, it becomes easier to consolidate power and authority by filling our head with distortions. Classic gaslighting.) And yet there is no significant body of research about gaslighting. It doesn't have a definition in the American Psychiatric Association's *Diagnostic and Statistical Manual of Mental Disorders* (DSM). It can look like several other disorders, such as narcissistic personality disorder, but I have found in my work as a therapist that gaslighters have a unique set of behaviors, and it behooves us to know them. Some gaslighters are easy to spot; others fly just under the radar. They are master manipulators and we need to know how to spot them, how to avoid them, and what to do if we're entangled with them.

THE ORIGINS OF THE TERM

What does *gaslighting* really mean, and where did it come from? The term *gaslight*, as a kind of psychological manipulation, was first added to the *Oxford English Dictionary* in December 2004, although the documented use of this word and its variants goes back to 1952 (Yagoda 2017). In fact, the term seems to have been coined by Patrick Hamilton in his 1938 play *Gas Light*, and first made popular by the 1944 movie *Gaslight*, directed by George Cukor and starring Ingrid Bergman and Charles Boyer. Gregory, Paula's husband, tries to convince her that she is going crazy—losing objects precious to her, hearing and seeing things that aren't there, thinking the lights are flickering when he claims they are not. It turns out it has all been a setup to "gaslight" her. I'll leave the rest for you to discover if you haven't seen the film.

Gaslighters use your own words against you; plot against you, lie to your face, deny your needs, show excessive displays of power, try to convince you of "alternative facts," turn family and friends against you—all with the goal of watching you suffer, consolidating their power, and increasing your dependence on them.

Interestingly enough, gaslighting is practiced equally by both genders. You are more likely to hear about male gaslighters, as female gaslighters' behaviors are sometimes not taken as seriously as they should be. For simplicity's sake, throughout this book I switch pronouns, using "he" or "him" and "she" or "her," or plurals to reflect that the information here applies to both genders.

For the gaslighters, manipulation is a way of life. Of course, it's important to note that manipulation in and of itself is not a bad thing. People use manipulation in positive ways all the time, and they can be great influencers of others (Cialdini 2009). For instance, we can be influenced and manipulated to work for a cause or take better care of ourselves. I guess you might call this persuasion, but it's a fine line. Gaslighters, however, use manipulation to gain control over others. There is no higher good to this kind of influence.

The manipulation is usually insidious and slow, and you may not even realize the extent of the damage until you have an "aha!" moment, your family or friends confront you, or a gaslighter is instrumental at getting you fired from your job. The goal of gaslighters is to keep you off-kilter and questioning your reality. The more you rely on them for the "correct" version of reality, the more control they have over you. This power and control is what gaslighters crave.

As mentioned, gaslighting shares characteristics of other personality disorders. Some people who gaslight meet the American Psychiatric Association's *DSM* criteria for the following disorders, known in the manual as Cluster B Personality Disorders:

- Histrionic Personality Disorder
- Narcissistic Personality Disorder
- Antisocial Personality Disorder
- Borderline Personality Disorder

All Cluster B personality disorders are characterized by impulsivity. Personality disorders are thought to be deeply ingrained in a person's behavior, making the individual very difficult to treat. People with personality disorders also experience being *ego-syntonic*—they believe everyone else is crazy or has a problem, not them. Sound similar to the gaslighters in your life? Even highly skilled psychotherapists have difficulty treating personality disorders. You cannot expect to be able to help (or get help for) some with a deep history of gaslighting. Usually the very best thing you can do is get as far away from them as possible. If that's not possible, creating really solid boundaries and not engaging them is next best. Throughout this book we'll look at how to do that, with the various types of gaslighters and situations where they'll find you.

If you are involved with a gaslighter, be it at home, work, or elsewhere, I hope you'll find some solace by knowing that you are not alone—and that in that feeling of unity with others, you will have the courage to distance yourself from the gaslighter in your life. You deserve better.

HOW I CAME TO THIS TOPIC

As a clinician in private practice, I have seen the effects of gaslighting up close and very personal. Because I specialize in ADHD, anxiety, and chronic pain, and gaslighters tend to target people with exactly these kinds of vulnerabilities, I tend to see more survivors of gaslighting than other therapists do. Quite a few of my clients experience depression, anxiety, and even suicidality as a result of a gaslighter's behavior.

I am also a Florida Supreme Court certified family mediator and circuit mediator. In mediations, I have seen gaslighters in action, particularly in custody disputes. Gaslighters are more likely to be involved in a custody fight; they also tend to draw out legal battles instead of trying to settle them. Seasoned attorneys and judges can usually pick up on gaslighting behaviors right away, but some gaslighters are so good at manipulation that even some mental health professionals miss it.

I see the kind of damage gaslighters can do, but I have also come to see their patterns of behavior. I started posting about gaslighting on my

Psychology Today blog and am receiving e-mails and calls from people all over the world. They were grateful to have language to speak about the hell of dealing with gaslighters in their lives and wanted to tell their stories. And they were asking for advice on how to protect themselves from or stop engaging with gaslighters.

One of my articles in particular, "11 Warning Signs of Gaslighting," posted in January 2017, went viral. It has received several million hits as of the printing of this book. After the post, the calls and e-mails escalated like wildfire. I was even contacted by people who recognized gaslighting behavior in themselves, and desperately sought help. The responses I received—from people so hungry for information—are a large part of what convinced me to write this book.

The more you educate yourself about gaslighting, the better you can protect yourself from it. Whether you are a victim/survivor of gaslighting; a therapist who helps people who have been impacted by gaslighting; a discoverer of your own gaslighting tendencies; or you are entering (or reentering) the dating world, starting a new job, or hiring employees and want to be proactive and warn yourself of potential red flags, you will find material of great value in this book.

WHAT'S AHEAD?

First, a note: as you'll see in this section, chapters are arranged thematically. That said, if you are tempted to flip to a chapter that seems particularly relevant to your situation, I strongly encourage you to start at the beginning and read the book all the way through. Gaslighting can be so complex, and you are likely to find wisdom for your situation in unexpected chapters. As you read about dating, parenting, work, and other places where gaslighters do their damage, a full picture of gaslighting, and what you can do about it, will emerge.

In Chapter 1, we will look at the clever processes of manipulation used by gaslighters. Gaslighting is essentially all about control, about gaining control over others—whether it is in the workplace, at home, or on a more global scale. You will learn how gaslighters use persuasion tactics to erode your self-esteem. Gaslighters ramp up their manipulation slowly. Once they see that you have accepted a slightly manipulated behavior, they know they've got you "locked in." They will then increase their manipulation of you, betting that you will continue to stick around. Gaslighters know that once you make a commitment to accepting a behavior, you will likely be much more consistent and compliant from then on.

Any intimate relationship can be challenging at times, but with gaslighters they are torturous. Even people who have a strong sense of self can get sucked into relationships with gaslighters and find it nearly impossible to leave. Chapter 2 helps you identify whether you are in a gaslighting relationship. You'll discover some of the obvious signs as well as more subtle ones, and see in stark terms the dangers of sticking around.

In Chapter 3, I will alert you to the red flags to look for on a first date and discuss the gaslighter's purpose in having a high-intensity courtship. I'll show you what actions you can take during the dating process to head off gaslighters at the pass. Finally, you will learn how to extricate yourself from an intimate relationship with a gaslighter if you find yourself in one, and how to protect yourself in the future.

In Chapter 4, we'll look at how gaslighters tear apart the workplace. Gaslighters will fabricate stories so as to get coworkers fired, harass and intimidate coworkers and employees, and pit coworkers against one another to divert attention from their own unethical workplace behaviors. Gaslighters can be anywhere within your company: employers, coworkers, or employees. They can be anyone from the CEO to a mailroom worker. We'll see how gaslighters have caused well-functioning companies to cave in, employees to run from their otherwise perfect jobs, and harassment lawsuits to be filed.

Gaslighters will often stop at nothing to make their coworkers look bad; they're only too happy to "throw someone under the bus." They'll steal credit for your work, give you a bad performance review to keep you in line, or threaten lawsuits as a way to get what they want. This may look a lot like harassment to you, and it is. But there are laws in the United Kingdom that can protect you from being harassed by a gas-lighter at work. And I will provide a list of tactics you can use to protect yourself, such as making sure you always have witnesses to any meetings with the gaslighter.

This is the era of #MeToo—people are speaking out about the harass-ment or abuse they have endured, which sometimes went on for years. What was previously dismissed or not talked about is now being spoken about openly. Gaslighters often harass others as a way to manipulate and gain control of them. Gaslighters tend to prey on people with less power and authority, and threaten those who may attempt to report their be-havior. Gaslighters can also be perpetrators of domestic violence—using verbal, financial, physical, sexual, and/or emotional abuse to keep their victims in a state of fear. In Chapter 5, I'll go over what makes up these different types of abuse—take a look and see whether any of them apply to your relationship. You'll learn why staying in an abusive relationship is so dangerous—and you'll learn the steps to getting out for good.

Gaslighters don't just work one on one. Gaslighting techniques are also used by people in power to keep citizens and opposition off-kilter, distracted, confused—in other words, easier to control. In Chapter 6, we'll turn our attention to the political arena and look at how some poli-ticians and dictators have gained a Svengali-like effect on citizens. This is gaslighting on the big stage.

Political gaslighters distract us with outrageous and outlandish behav-ior while dismantling long-standing cultural institutions and practices. What are citizens to do when the leader of their country is manipulating the public wholesale? In this chapter, we'll discuss ways that citizens can make positive social change while protecting themselves from gaslight-ing leaders, both legally and in terms of personal safety. Organizing with others is one of the most effective ways citizens can fight gaslighting. Yes, there is power in numbers.

Chapter 7 takes a look at another form of mass gaslighting—cults and extremist groups. While you may think that cults are the stuff of made-for-TV movies, you'll still want to read this chapter, since it can apply to closed communities. Cult and extremist group leaders fit our profile of gaslighters to a T. They tend to be very charismatic, and they go to extremes to exert their control, often separating people from their family, controlling their possessions and choice of partners, their work, and their sense of reality. Religious cults are certainly the most well known—but we will look at other kinds of cults and extremist groups as well. Any organization that functions within a closed ecosystem of extremely curtailed personal freedoms probably qualifies as a cult or extremist group. We'll look at the classic signs that you or a loved one is dealing with a cult or extremist group, as well as how to protect yourself or your loved one, or get away.

Some of us learned about gaslighting as children—from parents who used these behaviors to control. In Chapter 8, we'll look at how to cope with a parent who is or was a gaslighter. You will learn how a gaslighting parent can affect their children into adulthood. We'll also take a look at how gaslighting behaviors are often passed generation to generation. Kids raised by gaslighters often use gaslighting tactics themselves, in their own intimate relationships and friendships. These behaviors are called "fleas"—from the saying "Lie down with dogs and you will end up with fleas."

Continuing to utilize coping skills learned from gaslighting parents can lead to a lifetime of strained and broken relationships. Since many gaslighting parents have personality disorders, and children mimic their behaviors, the children are often misdiagnosed with personality disorders, too (Donatone 2016).

Whereas some children of gaslighters grow up to be gaslighters themselves, some do not. In fact, some children of gaslighters develop the opposite of a gaslighting personality—they become codependent and parentified—they take on a parental role toward their own parent(s). For this reason, we'll also cover how to handle a situation where you are caretaking a gaslighting parent, and how to handle gaslighters when completely removing them from your life is not an option. You will also learn how to cope when your siblings or adult children are gaslighters. You can't always break off contact with these people as you can with co-workers and friends. You'll learn how to cope when your siblings gaslight you. You will learn more about the "golden child" and "scapegoat" and how these roles play out in your adult relationships with your siblings.

The word *frenemy* was probably invented for gaslighters. These are folks with whom you seem to have a friendship, but it is always fraught with competition and rivalry. In Chapter 9, you will learn about these "emotional vampires" in friendships who can suck a person's energy dry. Gaslighters will collect "ammunition" from you to use that information against you later. They'll treat your vulnerability, usually a healthy part of relationships, as a weakness to be exploited. Gaslighters are also notorious for "splitting"—pitting friends against each other—so the victim has to lean on the gaslighter for support. The chapter will include tips on what to do when gaslighters spread harmful rumors about you to others—a common tactic when gaslighters feel you distancing yourself.

In Chapter 10, we'll look at how to cope with a gaslighting ex or ex's new partner that you can never really cut off. If you have children with a gaslighter, not only can you never truly leave the person, but you see your children suffering as a result. Parental alienation, turning the children against a parent, is a common goal of gaslighters (Kraus 2016). One parental alienation tactic used by gaslighters is to have their children refer to the other parent by her first name or asking the other parent to refer to the children by new names, to create emotional distance between the other parent and her children (Warshak 2015).

Gaslighters will sometimes even falsify abuse allegations to gain custody of the children. It's not the children's welfare they're interested in—it's control of the children and a way to "punish" the other parent. I have seen lengthy court battles that leave the nongaslighting parent emotionally and financially bankrupt. This chapter discusses how you can protect your children and fight for their rights and mental health.

By this point in the book, you may realize that *you* have gaslighting behaviors—or you may have suspected as much from the start and that's why you are reading in the first place. Chapter 11 will offer you guidance and perspective if you think you have been gaslighting others. Help for gaslighting behavior includes seeking counseling and coming to terms with how you have manipulated and hurt those around you. You'll learn more about how being around gaslighters for any length of time can bring out gaslighting behaviors in you as a way to cope—this is especially true if your parents or a long-term partner were gaslighters.

And finally, in Chapter 12 we'll revisit counseling treatments for protecting yourself and healing from a gaslighter's behavior. I'll give you information on how to find the best mental health professional for you, including what questions you should ask when you call to make an appointment. You will learn about different talk therapy approaches, and which might work best for you. You'll find in-depth information on different types of talk therapy: client-centered therapy, cognitive-behavioral therapy, dialectical behavior therapy, acceptance and commitment therapy, and solution-focused therapy. You will also find techniques to relieve anxiety that you can practice on your own, without needing to see a clinician. Additionally, you'll discover whether individual or group therapy works best for you. I'll also give you information on meditation, and how it can help you heal from gaslighting. Meditation is a no-cost, easy-access way to really decrease your stress level and boost your power to cope.

At the back of the book you'll find numerous resources—books, websites, and contacts to help you cope with being gaslighted.

Throughout, you'll be hearing directly from people who have experienced gaslighting firsthand. For privacy and safety reasons, identifying details have been masked, names have been changed, and in some cases, stories have been blended.

Without further ado, let's get to it.

1

IS IT ME, OR IS IT YOU MAKING ME THINK IT'S ME?

Portrait of a Gaslighter

GASLIGHTERS HAVE A NUMBER OF CHARACTERISTICS THAT ARE IM- portant to know. The list you'll encounter in this chapter may seem long or overbroad. My purpose in breaking out this list is not to create a clinical definition so much as to draw a better picture of what gaslighting is, how it operates, and how you can spot it.

You may find yourself thinking, "Well, that could describe the dynamics between my sister and me sometimes, and she's not a gaslighter." What we're looking at here are patterns. When enough of these qualities are present and persistent in a person, chances are you are dealing with a gaslighter.

So, let's begin to paint our portrait.

Their Apologies Are Always Conditional

One of the first things people often notice about gaslighters is that they are masters of the "conditional apology." You know, when someone says, "I'm sorry you feel that way." That's not an apology; the other person is not taking responsibility for his behavior, he's simply manipulating you into *feeling* seen by acknowledging your feelings. Gaslighters will only apologize if they are trying to get something out of you. Even if they do give you an apology, if you listen carefully, you'll see that it's really a nonapology, and they'll usually only give it because you asked for one or because they were forced by a judge or mediator to do so.

> "I was hit with, 'I'm sorry I cheated, but if you were a better wife I wouldn't have looked for affection elsewhere.'"
>
> —*Toni, 56*

They Use Triangulation and Splitting

Gaslighters have a whole bag of tricks for manipulating people, but two of their favorites are triangulation and splitting, because driving a wedge between you and other people serves their need to dominate and control. Let's look at these two tactics. Gaslighters triangulate and split for the following reasons:

> "My coworker told me that my gaslighting boss said he was letting me go. Gee, it would have been nice if my boss had told me himself."
>
> —*James, 35*

- To pit people against each other
- To get people to align with them
- To avoid direct confrontation
- To avoid responsibility for their actions
- To smear your character
- To spread lies
- To create chaos

Triangulation

Triangulation is the psychological term for communicating with someone through other people. Instead of directly speaking to someone, gaslighters will go to a mutual friend, another coworker, a sibling, or another parent to get a message across. Triangulation behavior ranges from implied communication—"I really wish Sally would stop calling me," hoping the receiver will pass this message along to Sally, to blatant statements, such as "Please tell Sally to stop calling me." Both are manipulative and indirect.

> "My husband told me my mother-in-law wanted to tell me she didn't agree with how I parented my child. I told him she could come talk to me herself, and I refused to talk about it with him any further. This is part of a pattern of manipulation from her."
>
> —*Joanie, 30*

Splitting

Gaslighters also love to pit people against each other. This is known as splitting. It gives them a sense of power and control. An example of splitting would be lying to a one friend about another, saying that a mutual friend had said something unflattering about them.

Gaslighters are the ultimate agitators and instigators. They get a power blast from getting people riled up and fighting with each other. The gaslighters will then watch comfortably from the sidelines, the very fight that they caused.

Follow this simple rule: *Unless a person says something to you directly, assume that what you are told was said about you by that person is not true.*

Gaslighters know that splitting and triangulating will draw you closer to them—and distance you from the person they are pitting you against.

> "My ex told me my son said to him that I needed to back off, and that he promised my son he wouldn't say anything. I called my son and asked him if he was having any concerns, and if there was something he wanted to talk about. He said no, he was fine, and we chatted for a bit. I knew what would happen if I had talked 'through' my ex—total chaos."
>
> —*Maggie, 55*

They Use Blatant Attempts to Curry Favor

Gaslighters are also masters at buttering people up. They will use false flattery to get what they want from you. As soon as you fulfill their needs, they'll drop their mask of niceness. Trust your gut. If the friendliness seems forced or phony, beware.

They Expect Special Treatment

Gaslighters feel that standard societal rules, such as politeness, respect, and patience, don't apply to them—they are above these rules. For example, a gaslighter will expect his partner to be home precisely at a certain time and have dinner on the table when he gets home. If the partner doesn't fulfill this obligation, the gaslighter becomes irrationally angry and retaliates.

They Mistreat People Who Have Less Power

You can tell a lot about people by how they treat a person who has less power than they do. For example, look at how someone treats wait-staff at a restaurant. Does she bark her order at the server, or does she order politely? What happens when a dish comes out and it is not what the diner requested? Does she assertively but politely ask for a correction, or does she make a scene and yell at the server? Demeaning the server can be a symptom of gaslighting.

"My ex-boyfriend would tease my little brother, but not in a buddy-buddy kind of way. It was more 'I'm going to figure out your weak spots and expose them.'"

—Heidi, 29

Another indication of gaslighting is how people behave toward or discuss children and animals. There is a difference between being indifferent to children or animals and treating them with disdain. Gaslighters may tease and pick on people or creatures perceived as "lesser."

You may also find that gaslighters have issues with road rage. They see someone cutting them off or not using a turn signal as a personal affront. They are ready to get even and correct this "wrong" that has been done to them. This behavior puts other drivers and the gaslighters' other passengers in danger.

> "At dinner with my ex-girlfriend, she screamed at the server when he brought out the wrong meal."
>
> —Daniel, 28

They Use Your Weaknesses Against You

Many times, you'll begin a relationship with a gaslighter feeling very safe, so you do what any trusting human in what she thinks is a healthy relationship would do—you share your intimate thoughts and feelings with the person. This is normal, natural, a healthy part of developing a close relationship. However, notice that the gaslighter rarely reveals as much intimate information about himself. Meanwhile, the information you share will soon be getting used against you in fights—it becomes psychological ammunition. For instance, a confidence you shared with the gaslighter about your

> "When he saw me crying during an argument, he took it as a chance to pounce on me. He saw a weakness like animals see fresh blood."
>
> —Dominique, 30

conflicted relationship with your sister is now thrown back at you as, "No wonder we are arguing. Your sister can't stand you, either. You treat her the same way you treat me."

They Compare You to Others

Gaslighters also use comparison as a way of driving a wedge between people, thus gaining control. Parents who gaslight frequently compare their children to each other—and in unrealistic and blatant ways. The gaslighting parent usually has a "golden child" and a "scapegoat child." The former can do no wrong, whereas the latter can do no right. This pits siblings against each other, and these feelings of competition commonly extend into adulthood.

Your boss may say, "Why can't you produce like Jane? She comes in at eight every morning. If she can do it, so can you." You may always be on the losing end of a comparison, except if it is to denigrate your "competition." That is, gaslighters may sing your praises to others if their goal is to make those others look bad. Perfection is unattainable, no matter how hard you try to meet the gaslighter's unreasonable expectations.

They Are Obsessed with Their Accomplishments

Gaslighters often will boast about the things they have accomplished, such as how they got an employee-of-the-month award at work. Never mind that it was fifteen years ago! They will badger you when you don't react with enthusiasm and praise when they tell you once again about the time that they "dropped the mic" on someone. Gaslighters put an extreme amount of importance on their own accomplishments, however delusional these accomplishments and attributes may be.

"When my girlfriend and I get into a fight, she constantly reminds me of how she was class valedictorian and that somehow makes her smarter than me. Hello, that was almost 20 years ago, and you had, like, 15 people in your graduating class."

—Victor, 37

They Prefer to Associate with People Who Fawn Over Them

Friends who would confront gaslighters about their behavior have no place in the gaslighters' life. Gaslighters will associate only with people who put them up on a pedestal, the way they feel they deserve to be treated. The second gaslighters feel that you no longer admire and cater to them, they will drop you.

They Put You in a Double Bind

Double binds are situations in which you are forced to choose between two undesirable options, or you are given conflicting messages. For instance, your gaslighting spouse tells you that you need to lose weight, then serves various desserts that night at dinner. You are in a no-win situation. Gaslighters like to place people in emotional dilemmas—your uncertainty is a sign to them that they have control over you.

They Are Obsessed with Their Image

How dare you make gaslighters look bad! They will pay you back. Gaslighters are obsessed with how they look to others. They tend to spend a large amount of money on grooming products and a lot of time looking at themselves in the mirror. They may get upset when you touch their hair or use one of their grooming products. Perfection is their goal—and it is impossible to obtain. Some gaslighters will even forgo necessities to pay for cosmetic surgery and other appearance-enhancing procedures.

They Are Obsessed with *Your* Image

Not only can gaslighters be overly obsessed with how they look, they can also be very particular about how *you* look. Body weight tends to especially be a target for gaslighters. They will ridicule their partners about their weight and clothing choices. Gaslighters will buy outfits for their partners that they deem acceptable. The underlying message: you are not good enough.

They Con People

Everything is a game to gaslighters—and conning is an essential part of the game.

Gaslighters want to see how much they can swindle you, emotionally or financially. Gaslighters are also are not as smart as they think—they will openly brag about their cons. This is one thing that often leads to their downfall.

"My brother said he needed to borrow a thousand dollars for rent because he had hit a rough patch. He cried about how his life had fallen apart. I scraped the money together for him. I found out later he blew it all gambling."

—*Shawna, 35*

They Cause Fear in Others

Family and friends of a gaslighter may defend the gaslighter against people that have the audacity to call him out on his behavior, or may themselves avoid confronting the gaslighter. This occurs for two main reasons: (1) The friends and family have become accustomed to the gaslighter's behavior and consider it to be normal; and (2) they are protecting themselves from looking disloyal to the gaslighter. This is especially common in the children of gaslighters. You will learn more about parentification of gaslighters' children in Chapter 5. When family and friends experience the retaliation of the gaslighter, they learn to fear him and avoid confronting him at all costs.

> "I was with my class on a field trip, and one of the parent chaperones started yelling at a kid because he bumped into her. He was in sixth grade and having fun with his friends—it wasn't a personal slight. The chaperone's son, also a sixth grader, told the boy, 'Now you've made her mad.'"
>
> —*Alex, 30*

They Have a Bad Temper

Because gaslighters feel they are "owed" loyalty by others and because they have a fragile ego, any behavior is taken personally by gaslighters—with disastrous consequences to victims. Gun violence is a concern with gaslighters due to their hot tempers. In the United States, 8.9 percent of the population have both impulsive angry behavior and own firearms (Swanson et al. 2015).

> "He told my daughter she was worthless and she would be lucky to find someone stupid enough to marry her. What did she do to get him so angry? She told him to stop yelling at her."
>
> —*Nora, 45*

Gaslighters at first will try to quietly display this anger, as to keep up their facade of perfection. However, they can only keep up this fake display for so long. The first time you see the gaslighter drop that mask, it can be quite startling.

Punishment Doesn't Affect Them

People with Cluster B personality disorders, those higher in gaslighting behaviors, tend to have a different neuron-firing pattern than do other people when disciplined or punished. They also don't value rewards in the way other people do (Gregory et al. 2015). This means that punishment and rewards tend to have less of an effect, which results in gaslighters' being more likely to "do their own thing" without concern about reactions from others.

They Practice "Cognitive Empathy"

Gaslighters may seem to understand how you feel, but take a closer look and you'll notice a robotic quality to their expressions of empathy. Their reactions seem flat or prerecorded—there is no real emotion behind their words. Gaslighters are experts at using "cognitive empathy"—acting as if they have empathy without actually feeling it.

They Refuse Personal Responsibility

It is always someone else's fault. This is the gaslighters' mantra. As noted earlier, personality disorders have a feature called ego-syntonic behavior. This means that people with a personality disorder feel that they are normal and everyone else is crazy. They feel their behavior is perfectly acceptable and meets the needs of their ego. This is one of the reasons that people with personality disorders are so difficult to treat—they don't think anything is wrong with them or their behavior.

> "I was seeing a family for therapy, and the mother no longer wanted to attend sessions—she just wanted to have her kid come in so I could 'fix him.' But she was more than willing to call me at all hours telling me how horrible her son was. When I told her that attending her son's sessions was a condition of therapy, she said I was a terrible therapist."
>
> —Jason, 50

They Wear You Down over Time

Gaslighters bank on the idea that, with enough time, they can weaken your spirit. They also expect that if they gradually ramp up their manipulative behavior, you will be the proverbial frog in the frying pan. And so, they will increase the heat so slowly that you don't realize you're being psychologically burned alive. In the beginning of your relationship with a gaslighter, things may be pretty good—in fact, they are too good to be true. The gaslighter still even compliments you from time to time. Then, the criticisms creep in. The reason for this flip-flop between contempt and praise? Gaslighters know confusion weakens the psyche. With uncertainty comes vulnerability. Toward the end, you are believing blatant lies that you never would have accepted at the beginning of your relationship.

They Habitually Lie

If gaslighters are caught with the proverbial "hand in the cookie jar," they will look you right in the eye and tell you they did no such thing.

"My ex told me that I never saw any inappropriate texts on his phone. He actually said he thought I was losing my mind. I started to think maybe he was right."

—Audra, 29

It makes you question your sanity—*Maybe I didn't see them do that after all*. This is what they want—for you to become more dependent on their version of reality. They may even push things further along by telling you that you are losing your mind. What gaslighters say is virtually meaningless; they are habitual liars. For this reason, you always want to pay attention to what gaslighters do, not what they say.

They Are Terrible Teasers

Gaslighters are terrible teasers. At first, it's small things said when the two of you are alone, such as how your hair looks, or your accent. It

"My brother always calls me a loser. A few times, fine. But then he did it in front of girls I was interested in, and his voice would get really mean-sounding. I told him it wasn't cool to do that, and he just blew it off, like, 'Deal with it.'"

—Javier, 25

then ramps up to their teasing you in front of your friends. When you say that their comments or mimicry bothers you, they tell you that you are being too sensitive. This is different than just regular sibling teasing or joking around with friends. With gaslighters, it is a perpetual teasing, it has a mean quality to it, and most important, your requests for it to stop go unheeded.

Their Compliments Aren't Really

The gaslighter is a pro at giving out "compliments," a portmanteau of *compliment* and *insult*. There is no such thing as a true compliment with a gaslighter (or narcissist). It is always backhanded or passive-aggressive (see page 208).

> "He said that the dinner I cooked was really good . . . . and that he was glad he finally taught me how to cook. I went from feeling good to feeling terrible in a couple of seconds."
>
> —*Mila, 23*

They Project Their Emotions

Gaslighters may have such a poor sense of their own emotions or actions that they have no idea they are projecting their behavior onto someone else. For example, a gaslighter will say you need a drug test, when he, himself, is the one who is using.

They Isolate You

Gaslighters tend to tell you that your friends and family are bad influences on you, or that you don't seem happy when you are around those you actually care about. They may also refuse to go to family events with you because "Your family makes me uncomfortable" or some other vague, substance-less excuse. Such a gaslighter is banking on the idea that instead of having to explain to your family why you are attending holiday events without him, you'll end up spending the occasion alone with him. The more the gaslighter succeeds at isolating you, the more susceptible you are to his control.

They Use "Flying Monkeys"

Gaslighters will try to send messages to you through other people—especially when you take the courageous step to cut off contact. These people are sometimes unwittingly carrying a gaslighter's messages. You will learn more about flying monkeys in Chapter 2.

They Tell Others That You Are Crazy

Gaslighters will drive wedges between you and other people in all sorts of clever ways. After you leave a job with a gaslighting boss, for instance, your colleagues might tell you that they wondered what was going on, because the boss told them to "tread lightly around that one." There is no more effective way to discredit you than to tell people that you are crazy. You are now seen as fragile and unstable.

They Don't Keep Promises

> "My ex-boyfriend told me his boss said he could relocate when I got a new job across the country. But when my new job was confirmed, my ex said his boss took back the offer. This wasn't the first time he changed his story when things got down to the wire."
>
> —Jerusha, 28

For gaslighters, promises are made to be broken. If gaslighters promise you anything, assume that it is an empty promise. If a gaslighter happens to be your employer, get those promises in writing. You'll learn more about gaslighting in the workplace in Chapter 4.

Loyalty Is Required—But Not Reciprocal

Gaslighters require complete and unrealistic loyalty—but don't expect loyalty from them. As you'll learn in Chapter 2, they are notorious for their compulsive infidelity. Gaslighters do whatever they want to you, but God help you if they think you've betrayed them. They will make your life a living hell.

They Kick People When They Are Down

Not merely satisfied to leave well enough alone when they have inflicted their damage, gaslighters continues to beat those who are on the ground. They get a sick pleasure from watching others suffer. They especially get excited when they know someone is suffering *because of them*.

They Avoid Admitting Problems They've Caused

Gaslighters will say that you, or people around them, are irrational and have things all wrong, when in reality they are avoiding having to explain themselves or take responsibility for their actions. For example, gaslighters will put their coworkers at risk by not following workplace safety guidelines. When they are confronted by superiors about these violations, they argue that no one really got hurt, and that they are being unfairly targeted. Or gaslighting parents who are told by their child's teacher that it would be helpful if they would spend more time on reading at home, will automatically blame the other parent for the child's issues with reading, or blame the teacher or the school for bringing it up.

They Bait and Switch

Your gaslighter boss comes by your cubicle and asks whether you have a couple of minutes to chat about a new project. You are excited, especially because this extra work might be an incentive for the boss to give you a raise. In the meeting with your boss, you're told that you do have a new project—because someone else was let go. Now you have additional responsibility without reward. Before you can ask any questions, the boss tells you he is busy, and closes the door behind you. This is a classic manipulation move—bring people in by promising them one thing, then switch it on them once they accept it.

BUT DON'T PEOPLE JUST MANIPULATE OTHERS SOMETIMES?

What's the difference between someone who manipulates for a particular benefit, and a gaslighter? It's a fine line. Whereas manipulation (or influence) is an essential part of some jobs, such as sales, it's a pattern of behavior with gaslighters—their default mode. That is, when most people lie, it's for a specific outcome—to avoid confrontation, get ahead, or curry favor with someone. But with gaslighters, there is no particular reason to lie and yet they do it over and over again, often in an escalating fashion as they feel the effects of their power. This is done just for the sake of doing it—to con, gain control of, and confuse you. Gaslighters manipulate others not just situationally but as a way of life.

WHY DO GASLIGHTERS BEHAVE THIS WAY?

For gaslighters, everything they do is about gaining power over others and filling their endless pit of neediness. There is a debate regarding "nature vs. nurture" with gaslighters. Sometimes people are just born manipulators. Gaslighting behaviors can also be learned from parents or other people in a child's life. Gaslighters who were psychologically abused as children learned maladaptive coping techniques so as to cope with the cruelty inflicted upon them. In Chapter 7 you will learn more about gaslighters in the family.

Many gaslighters have *narcissistic injury*—a perceived threat to their self-worth or self-esteem. They then react with narcissistic rage. This rage isn't always loud—it can be quiet and just as dangerous. In fact, when the narcissist is full of rage, it usually comes across as an eerie calm—enough to make the hairs on the back of your neck stand up.

WHY HAVE YOU LIVED WITH THIS?

It takes a certain amount of *cognitive dissonance* to remain connected to a gaslighter—whether it is a partner, sibling, parent, coworker, or someone you helped elect. Cognitive dissonance occurs when you have information about the gaslighter that is completely contradictory to your beliefs, values, and what you thought you knew about that person. When we have a state of cognitive dissonance, we react in one of the following ways:

- We ignore the contradictory information.
- We fight against the contradictory information.
- We replace our beliefs and values with the contradictory information.

You may have put up with it because you convinced yourself that it was normal. But the healthiest way to resolve cognitive dissonance is to take action to bring yourself back into alignment with your own beliefs and values—and many times that means leaving or distancing yourself from the gaslighter. You will learn more in this book about how to do this in a healthy way—even if you have to have some form of ongoing contact with the gaslighter, such as in a coparenting relationship.

SO, WHAT CAN YOU DO?

Throughout this book we'll look at ways to decrease a gaslighter's influence in your life. Many of these will boil down to one thing: get as far away as possible. Because gaslighters are so slippery and manipulative, your best bet is to cut off all contact. If you can't completely cut off contact, drastically reduce it. Also, never let them see you sweat. Gaslighters' payoff is knowing they've upset you. If you don't react or act bored, they will usually leave you alone.

Some people try giving a gaslighter "a taste of his own medicine" by yelling and manipulating right back. This can work in the very short term, shocking the gaslighter into silence, but don't be fooled. He'll come back for revenge. This is a tricky game to play. And at what cost to you? In Chapter 7, we'll look at what it means to have "fleas"—to take on the gaslighter's behaviors. It doesn't work. You don't want to start acting like a gaslighter, no matter how strong the temptation.

IF YOU'VE FORGOTTEN HOW HEALTHY PEOPLE BEHAVE . . . .

If you've been around a gaslighter for a while, it can be easy to forget what a psychologically healthy person looks like. Psychologically healthy people:

- Encourage expression of opinions
- Say what they mean and mean what they say
- Support you even if they don't agree with you

- Let you know in a direct and kind way if you've hurt them
- Are capable of emotional intimacy—the mutual sharing of feelings and ideas
- Trust others
- Exhibit behaviors that are genuine and authentic

LET'S MOVE ON to how gaslighting works in dating and intimate relationships. So many good, smart, loving people find themselves with gaslighters, and I want to show you that there are ways out. You don't have to live your life under their spell.

2

LOVE-BOMBED, HOOVERED, DEVALUED, AND DISCARDED

Gaslighting in Intimate Relationships

O NE OF THE MOST COMMON PLACES YOU'LL FIND GASLIGHTING IS IN intimate relationships. Gaslighters are very seductive. They will sweep you off your feet (we call this *love-bombing*—more to follow)—and then drop you off a cliff. But the initial seduction is so strong that when things do go south, it's hard not to feel that you're to blame or that somehow you should be able to get that wonderful person back.

But that's not the way it works with the gaslighter. The initial charm is all part of the game. There is no getting that wonderful person back. He doesn't exist.

As noted in the Introduction, both women and men can be gaslighters. In fact, as far as we know, the genders are represented equally. One reason we tend to think of gaslighting as a male "sport," is that men are often more reluctant (perhaps embarrassed) to talk to someone about a female partner who is being emotionally abusive. Other times, when they do feel the need and build up the courage to talk about it, they are not believed.

One of my aims here is to correct this view. Men who are being gaslighted by women are just as entitled to relief and good support as women are! Not to mention that gaslighting happens in LGBTQ relationships, too.

> "I caught him cheating, and he said, 'We never agreed to be monogamous.'"
>
> —Ted, 50

Relationships with gaslighters are filled with tumult—so much so that it's easy to feel shame. But being attracted to a gaslighter is no cause for shame. Even brilliant, successful, and otherwise discerning people can be easily seduced by a gaslighter's many initial charms. With the tools and insights in this chapter, you'll be able not only to discern whether you are in a relationship with a gaslighter but discover some strategies for getting away.

With a gaslighter, once the behavior emerges, there is rarely a calm moment. You are constantly wondering what you did to upset him. You can't figure out what's wrong, and maybe you turn to the Internet for help but can't find it. Your family and friends are concerned for you. And all the while, the gaslighter is telling you that your family and friends are up to no good, that you need to get away from them. (It's all part of his snare.)

How could something that started out so wonderfully go so wrong?

Because gaslighters are masters at hooking people in—and then tossing them out. They know how to give you whiplash like you've never had before.

YOU MEAN IT'S NOT MY FAULT?

It often comes as a great relief when I tell my clients that they are not to blame! It's very normal for people to blame themselves for their partners' behavior. *If I was a good person, she wouldn't have acted that way.* It is also normal, when you're dealing with gaslighters, to *be* blamed for things *they* are doing. This is classic projection.

> "This whole time I thought I did something to make him act like this."
>
> —Charmaine, 28

A good example of gaslighting projection is when a cheater constantly accuses his spouse of cheating. The gaslighter will say things like "I know you and your coworker have something going on the side" or "I saw you flirting with him" or "I see you wear that skimpy dress when you go out with your friends. Planning on meeting someone?" when in fact it is the gaslighter who is cheating all along.

Gaslighters turn reality on its head. This is definitely one to watch out for. If you find yourself blaming yourself for your partner's poor behavior or treatment of you, please consider alternative perspectives. More on how to do this throughout the book.

> "It's not my fault she acted that way?"
>
> —John, 43

GASLIGHTERS AND SEX

Gaslighters are very good at pretending at romantic behavior and connection at the beginning of your relationship, but they can't keep it up forever. They quickly become very one-sided with sex. It's all about their pleasure, not yours. You just happen to be there; you are the means to an end. Pretty soon you feel more like an object than a partner who is loved and cherished.

Gaslighters will also often set up "rules" for sex, spoken or unspoken, such as:

- You should always be available for sex when they want it.
- If you want to have sex, they will probably tell you no.
- They will withhold sex as a way to punish you.
- If you want to receive oral sex, you have to earn it.
- If you don't give them what they want sexually, they will belittle you.
- They'll tell you they would be more sexually attracted to you if you changed your appearance.
- They don't really care if you aren't feeling pleasure.
- And they don't really care if you are feeling pain.

Very often, if you tell a gaslighter no to a particular sex act, you'll be pressured into doing it anyway. Pressuring could be anything from

"You're so good at it" to actually forcing you to engage in sex or particular sexual activities.

Gaslighters also don't take kindly to being turned down for sex. As a punishment, they will tell you they are never going to initiate it with you again—as a way to "teach" you the correct way to behave. For more on gaslighting as it relates to sexual assault and abuse, see Chapter 5.

Infidelity and the Gaslighter

Here are a couple of examples of how gaslighting works when it comes to infidelity:

John, forty-three, hired an assistant at his office, Jane. John's wife, Mary, was convinced John and Jane were having an affair, even though John said they were strictly colleagues, and he couldn't figure out why Mary would think he was cheating. Mary started cyberstalking Jane and making threatening phone calls to her—to the point that Jane filed a restraining order against Mary. Mary also became physically abusive to John—at one point she threw a heavy vase close to his head. She then commented that if she'd *really* wanted to hurt him, she would have aimed closer to his head. Mary told John that Jane had called her several times, detailing information about their supposed affair. When John asked what Jane had said, Mary responded, "Wouldn't you like to know? I've learned enough." John blamed himself for Mary's out-of-control behavior. He felt he must have done *something* to instigate Mary's actions because they were so extreme.

Mary's behavior was more than just irrational jealousy. She was gaslighting both Jane and John to maintain power over her husband, particularly when he wasn't home with her.

Even if John *had been* cheating on Mary, her reaction was extremely out of proportion. Healthy people do not stalk and harass others, regardless of what "bad" behavior they think their spouse has committed. John began attending individual therapy for several months at the urging of his sister. He realized that he had been in an abusive marriage, and took steps to leave Mary. After John moved out of the house, Mary never spoke to him again. All divorce proceedings were done directly through her attorney. Later, John worked in therapy on learning red flags to watch out for when he started dating again.

Brian noticed Sarah had been coming home from work later than usual in the past month. She used to come home at seven p.m., but now she regularly arrived home at nine, with not so much as a returned phone call or text. Brian waited another month before he asked Sarah what was going on at work. He even asked her point blank whether she was having an affair. He would have asked her earlier, but he was afraid she would become icy cold and shut him out, as she had done several times during their marriage.

When asked, Sarah responded coolly that she wasn't sure what Brian was talking about, that she had always gotten home from work at the same time. She then said that she had been concerned about John's state of mind lately, and wondered whether he was the one having an affair. Brian never brought up the late nights to Sarah again, although he thought about it constantly. He even convinced himself that Sarah might have been right. Maybe she had always come home at that time.

Sarah told Brian he needed to go to therapy "to figure out why you feel the need to persecute me." She attended one session with him but was bristling from the start, telling the therapist that she wasn't sure what was wrong with Brian but that he needed to figure it out or she was leaving him. Then, Sarah started coming home reeking of liquor. Brian tried to push his thoughts of Sarah's behavior out of his head. However, one night he caught Sarah in an intimate phone call. When confronted, she denied having an affair. Brian finally learned the truth when the wife of one of Sarah's coworkers contacted him. It turns out that Sarah and this woman's husband had been having an affair for at least six months. As Sarah left the home for good, her parting words to Brian were, "If you were a better husband, I wouldn't have had to seek companionship elsewhere." Brian wondered why he hadn't just "cut and run" when he was first dating Sarah and she admitted she was living with her boyfriend. He realized, in retrospect, that he'd liked the fact that he'd "won" Sarah when she decided to move in with him. But now he realized that Sarah's cheating and then jumping into a new relationship was a red flag. In the future, he would look for these warning signs before making a commitment. He also worked at learning why he was attracted to someone like Sarah.

There are some key features to these stories that I see over and over again with survivors of gaslighting (Sarkis 2017). Gaslighting spouses (or partners):

- Are caught cheating, and their spouse doesn't bring it up due to fears of violence and/or retaliation
- Have a history of cheating in previous relationships
- Openly flaunt their cheating, relatively sure that their spouse won't confront them
- Project their cheating onto their spouse. This acts as a distractor from the gaslighter's cheating.
- Change routines and behaviors to hide cheating or substance abuse, and then deny these changes when asked.
- Respond to a perceived "bad" behavior from their spouse in a way grossly out of proportion to the event. This response can include stalking and threatening behaviors.
- If in couple's therapy, tell the therapist that it is their spouse's fault, and imply or outright state that the spouse needs to "be fixed" for the marriage to continue
- Have been sending up red flags from the time the couple started dating, but their spouse either wasn't aware that these were warning signs, or chose to ignore them
- Blame their spouse for their own cheating, often claiming that the spouse has not been fulfilling their needs
- Never apologize, yet expect an apology *from* their spouse
- Are delusional in their views of being "wronged"

- Immediately drop their spouse if accused or found out, refusing to communicate with the spouse—almost as if the spouse dropped off the face of the earth

I cannot emphasize this enough: No one *causes* a spouse (or partner) to cheat. *You didn't cause your spouse to cheat.* Your spouse cheated of his own free will. Your spouse had options—including talking to you if he had any concerns about the relationship, making an effort to attend couple's therapy, or simply discontinuing the relationship. *Cheating was a choice he made.*

It is also important to note that your spouse did not cheat because you were lacking something, no matter what your spouse says. Your spouse cheated because gaslighters crave newness and attention. Even if you could do "everything perfectly," whatever that means, the gaslighter still has a bottomless pit of need that can never be filled. You would be blamed for the cheating no matter what.

Taking personal responsibility is not a characteristic of gaslighters—they always believe it is someone else's fault. And they rarely feel empathy or remorse. This is another example of *ego-syntonic* behavior that I mentioned earlier.

If you discover that a gaslighting partner has been unfaithful, make sure you get tested for sexually transmitted diseases (STDs). The gaslighter, although he may have told you otherwise, really doesn't care about your well-being, including your sexual health. He most likely did not use protection when he was cheating. You were the furthest thing from his mind.

For more research on where to get low-cost STD testing, see the Resources section at the end of this book.

LOVE-BOMBING, HOOVERING, AND STONEWALLING

When Josie met Jamie, it was love at first sight. On their first date, Jamie said to her, "I know this is really early to say something like this, but I think we could be together for a long time." Jamie showered Josie with gifts and trips, telling her, "I've never felt this way about anyone." Jamie talked with Josie about marriage and kids within their first week of dating. Josie described feeling "high" from Jamie's attention. She wound up spending all her time with him, and eventually stopped seeing her other friends. Jamie said they were "bad influences" on Josie and constantly reminded her that she was happier when she wasn't around them. "I had never been treated with so much adoration—I was put up on a pedestal."

After a few months of "bliss," Josie started experiencing Jamie's stonewalling. He would completely ignore her, without Josie's knowing what she had done to upset him. She would wrack her brain trying to figure it out. Jamie wouldn't return calls, "which made me worried and made me contact him more."

Josie's sister told her she needed to stop contacting Jamie and wait for him to contact her. "It was one of the hardest things for me to do, because I still didn't know what I did wrong." Josie now spent her time waiting for Jamie to call and scouring the Internet for articles on what to do when your partner ignores you.

Two weeks later, she got a text from Jamie. It said, "Your bike is here." Josie said her heart raced and she got butterflies in her stomach. She answered his text right away. "Are you okay? Where are you?" This was met with more silence. After some heavy crying, she texted, "I can't do this. I just don't understand anymore."

A few hours later, she got a knock on her door. It was Jamie, with her bike—and flowers. "He told me that we needed to go bike riding together, like, *right now*. I felt really uncomfortable about it, but I went anyway." During the bike ride, Jamie didn't mention anything about his disappearing or lack of communication—instead, he talked about moving in together. "It was like nothing had happened at all. I chalked it up to him just needing some space."

About two months after they reconciled, Jamie started the silent treatment again—and it went off and on like this for two years. The times in between the stonewalling became "worse and worse. We stopped having what I called 'honeymoon' periods." Jamie went from asking her to move in with him to saying he had changed his mind "because I was unstable. He kept me hanging in there with his promises that we would take things to the next level. Then it would fall apart again."

Josie said of Jamie, "Looking back, Jamie looked great on paper—smart, educated, funny . . . . but now that I really look at it, there were some red flags from the beginning. He had cut off contact with his brother and sister several years prior, and he was always blaming people at work for why he never got a promotion. He also criticized me more and more over time, especially for things I couldn't change—like my family."

Love-Bombing

Gaslighters are amazingly good at keeping their pathology in check until they know you are hooked. The first time your partner blatantly lies, you think you must have misheard him; after all, the person who was showering you with love just wouldn't do that. But he will, and he will continue to blatantly lie. Gaslighters erode your perception of reality until you feel you cannot function normally without them.

Love-bombing is a way that gaslighters get you hooked. In the case of Josie and Jamie, Jamie showered Josie with gifts and told her everything he knew she wanted to hear about the kind of future they'd have together. Jamie also quickly zeroed in on getting a commitment from Josie. When a gaslighter love-bombs you, it is hard to get away. The attention you receive is intoxicating. It's like nothing you have experienced before. Finally, you think, someone is treating you the way you want to be treated. That pedestal he puts you on feels damn good. But eventually you will always fall off it, and it is a long way down.

Hoovering

With gaslighting, we also use the term *hoovering* to describe the way gaslighters will suck you back in if they feel you checking out. (Yes, it comes from the vacuum of the same name.) When Jamie cut off contact with Josie, and when Josie stopped reaching out to him, he swooped in immediately—and started talking about moving in together. If gaslighters get any inkling of perceived abandonment, they work at sucking you back in. They put on the full-court press to get you back in their clutches.

Nothing causes fear in gaslighters more than the feeling of abandonment. This abandonment is what is known as a *narcissistic injury*. Gaslighters have an endless pit of need—a need for attention. No matter what you do, you will never be humanly capable of fulfilling gaslighters' needs. They will always turn to something or someone else to fill that void. When they find that something or someone else to transfer their attention to, they will drop you like the proverbial hot potato. It is heartbreaking and confusing. When you first see a gaslighter's facade crack, it can be startling to see who is really underneath.

It's very normal to feel like it is your fault for not noticing the instability of a gaslighter earlier in your relationship. However, keep in mind that gaslighters are masters at acting "normal." In fact, *love-bombing* is just an exaggerated form of what most people do when dating and starting a relationship. You're attracted to each other and feel excitement. The difference is, in a healthy relationship you each still retain your own identity and activities. You *want* but don't *need* the other person. In love-bombing, that wooing is cranked up to an extreme level. The gaslighter wants you to need him to be the kind of person he is projecting on to you; he wants to make sure you don't see the insecure person underneath.

With hoovering, gaslighters give you just enough to string you along. It can be in the form of suggesting, if not outright promising, something you'd like. If in the beginning of your relationship the two of you talked about getting married and this has never materialized when you bring it up, all of a sudden after stonewalling the gaslighter starts saying maybe he's ready. In Josie's case, it was Jamie's talk about moving in together. Be aware: these plans never materialize. The gaslighter knows just how to get you hooked back in with the promise of something you want.

Often, gaslighters also will use objects to reel you back in. You will get texts and e-mails about things he has of yours. He'll say, "I have your stuff. Come get it or it's going to the curb" or "Do you want your chair/

bike/clothes?" Be aware that it is not the gaslighter's intention to give you back these items and then leave you alone—it is just a pretense to get back in contact with you.

Hoovering also involves gaslighters' wanting physical contact. Don't be surprised if the sex is better than ever. It appears your gaslighter is actually connecting with you emotionally. Giving you the physical contact you have craved is another way the gaslighter strings you along and gets you hooked again. It won't last.

One of the most confusing parts of a relationship with a gaslighter is that it isn't 100 percent bad. Just as in any other abusive relationship. When the gaslighter is hoovering, it actually feels pretty good, almost as good as the person behaved toward you in the beginning of your relationship. When things are going this way, it's hard to remember that the hoovering is a means to an end. But it is. It will stop.

> "I actually had to ask her for an apology. And even then it was, 'I'm sorry you're so sensitive.'"
>
> —Liz, 60

As with all gaslighting, it's about seeing the behavior *patterns* and knowing when you're being had.

Stonewalling

I've used the word *stonewalling* a few times already in this chapter without explaining it. Stonewalling is the disappearing act or radio silence gaslighters will treat you to when they get caught and feel that they have been "done wrong," or just prefer to not talk about something because it's more convenient for them that way. If you don't live with them, you won't see or hear from them. They will not answer texts or calls. Meanwhile, you grow more anxious the longer you don't hear from them. In the case of Josie and Jamie, Jamie would stonewall Josie; he'd just stop communicating with her and disappear for periods of time, then reappear when he wanted to.

Does it bother gaslighters that their silence is tormenting you? Far from it. They love that their behavior causes you to get upset. If you live with a gaslighter, stonewalling can get so bad that the gaslighter acts as if you don't exist—even when you are right in front of him.

What's the best way of dealing with stonewalling? Go radio silence yourself. Don't let on that stonewallers' behavior bothers you. Again, they are seeking a reaction. Don't give it to them. Carry on as if their behavior makes not one iota of difference in your life. Because in reality, it doesn't. Remember, gaslighters don't have any real power over you.

GETTING OUT OF A RELATIONSHIP WITH A GASLIGHTER

Getting counseling is imperative when you are considering ending a relationship with a gaslighter, or have already done so. You may feel isolated, helpless, anxious, and depressed. These are all very common feelings when leaving someone who is abusive. You may continue having these feelings for quite a while after you have left a gaslighter. You are learning how to rebuild your self-concept, your self-esteem, and your life. For more information on counseling, see Chapter 12.

> "I stayed with him and defended him because I didn't understand what his behavior was doing to me. He's highly intelligent, and was able to get away with stalking me when he manipulated the police."
>
> —*Daisy, 50*

Here comes the tough love. If you are in a relationship with a gaslighter, you need to end it. It is an abusive relationship, and it will not improve. You need to get out. Please, please do the following, with the support of family and friends if you can:

- Set up blocking rules on your e-mail. Block all her e-mail addresses.
- Block calls and texts from her phone.
- Block calls from her friends.
- Block calls from her parents.
- Unfriend and block her on social media.
- Unfriend people who may report your activities and whereabouts to the gaslighter.
- If possible, move to a part of town where you are less likely to run into her.
- If you can't move, avoid places you know she frequents.

You need to end this relationship. This cannot be stressed enough. Things will only get worse with the gaslighter. So maybe this time, you didn't get an STD from her cheating on you . . . . but what about the next time? If you stay, it's almost guaranteed there will be a next time. In addition, if you hang in there, the gaslighter will have proof that she can take advantage of you and you will stay—resulting in more cheating.

"It's so hard to leave. So hard. To someone else, it might be easy, 'he treats you like crap, leave.' But you get to a point where you think you literally can't survive without him."

—Winnie, 53

Leaving the gaslighter is a very trying process. It may feel close to impossible to you right now. You would think leaving a gaslighter would be a relief—but instead it causes you the most heartache you've experienced in a relationship. How could you be so deceived? Are all women/men like this? The answer is no. They are not all like this.

There is a bright future awaiting you. This relationship is not nurturing your soul or helping you become a better person. It is sucking your energy dry and increasing your depression and anxiety. You are not the person you were when you entered this relationship. Wouldn't you like to get back to being that bright, vibrant person? It is possible.

Moving Out

If you have items in the gaslighter's home (or your shared home), have someone else collect them for you. You can also have the police accompany you. First, ask yourself whether you *really* need those items. Are they valuable or do they have particular significance for you? If the answer is no, consider that maybe they're just the price you have to pay to regain your sanity. Also, be honest with yourself. Do you really need that stuff,

"I honestly don't know what I would have done without the help of legal aid. They helped me protect myself and my kids when I left him . . . . I wasn't sure how I was even going to get through the day."

—Sherise, 36

or are you maybe looking for a way to stay connected with the gaslighter? As I suggested earlier, a gaslighter can be like a drug, and you may be looking for a fix. Any contact with the gaslighter opens up the chance you'll get sucked back in. And the pattern will never change. It's hard but for your health and well-being you need to stay strong and disconnect.

If you are staying in the residence, have someone with you when the gaslighter removes his belongings. The police department can have someone present for your protection and the safety of your property. This is especially important if the gaslighter has firearms in your home. The police can secure the firearms before any other moving begins. Where possible, follow these precautions:

- Call the police's nonemergency number to ask for a police officer to be present while your former partner moves his belongings out. If your former partner has firearms, let the police know, and they can make sure they are moved out of the home securely.
- Put the gaslighter's belongings in the garage or another location, such as a rented storage unit, so he has limited access to your home.
- Change your locks and door codes immediately.
- If you live in a gated area or have a doorman or household help, alert such staff that from now on this person should not be let into the premises for any reason. Provide a name and photo. If you feel uncomfortable about doing this, be assured that gate guards and doormen consider protecting you as part of their job.
- Change the password on your wireless router and on your e-mail and other online accounts.
- Consider installing webcams and other forms of security. Some gaslighters have been known to hack into accounts, stalk their exes, and "test" security systems.
- Remove your name and contact information from online information search engines. For more information on these sites, see the Resources section at the end of this book.

If you feel that you or your family members' lives are in danger, contact your court about getting a restraining order against the gaslighter. A restraining order, granted by a judge, states that a person cannot contact you and cannot be within a certain distance of you or your home. This order does not protect a gaslighter from stalking you or threatening you, but you can report the behavior to the police, and the gaslighter can be arrested for violating the restraining order. It can be quite difficult for victims of gaslighters to completely stay away from the gaslighter, due to the gaslighter's influence on victims. However, victims also need to follow the guidelines of the restraining order, and not contact the gaslighter—under any circumstances. For more information on restraining orders, see the Resources section at the end of this book.

Keep documentation. If your ex contacts you directly or through others, write down the date, time, and exact events, including direct quotes. Notetaking apps or a notebook can be helpful for keeping track of this information. If you have to get the police or an attorney involved, presenting information kept all in one location will make the process much easier for you, and more helpful to them.

There are most likely pro bono (free) legal services available in your community, and domestic violence shelters may accept you. Abuse is abuse, whether it is emotional, verbal, or physical. For more information on pro bono legal services and domestic violence shelters, see the Resources section at the end of this book.

It is not uncommon after a breakup with a gaslighter to feel so despondent that you might try to hurt yourself. Gaslighters really excel at making you dependent on them, and breaking down your self-esteem and self-worth. If you are feeling as though you may hurt yourself, call the National Suicide Prevention Lifeline right now at 1-800-273-8255.

Flying Monkeys

Once you have left a gaslighter, well-meaning friends and relatives may approach you and tell you they think you should give him another chance. They may even tell you that you've always been too sensitive or difficult. Chances are, the gaslighter contacted these people to put them up to this. The people who willingly, and sometimes unwittingly, do the gaslighter's bidding are known as "flying monkeys." The term comes from the winged creatures who accompanied the Wicked Witch of the West in *The Wizard of Oz*. The gaslighter sends these messengers to guilt you back into the relationship. Common flying monkey statements include the following:

- I really think you should give him another chance.
- I'm sure he really didn't mean those things. You know you can be difficult sometimes.
- He's really upset right now. I think you should call him.
- He said he's throwing the rest of your stuff on the street.
- The two of you were really good together.
- I heard he's interested in someone that might be perfect for him.

Be very clear with these sometimes well-meaning people that you will not talk with them about your ex under any circumstances. If flying monkeys bring up your ex again, shut them down immediately. In extreme cases, you may need to limit or cut off your contact with the flying monkeys as well.

Children

If you have children with the gaslighter, rest assured that in Chapter 8 we will discuss what to do. There are solutions for these situations where you are not able to fully cut off contact. For example, hiring or having a parent coordinator appointed for you can help you navigate the co-parenting relationship.

Pets

If you share a pet with a gaslighter, take your pet with you—even if you got the pet together. Your pet's well-being is at stake. Gaslighters will use a pet as a tool to get you back. They may even hurt or threaten to hurt a pet as a way to get revenge or attention. Contact the police and an attorney if the gaslighter refuses to give you your pet.

It is possible the gaslighter has already abused your pet. As you learned in Chapter 1, gaslighters have little true regard for the feelings or suffering of other living things. Never leave your pet alone with a gaslighter. There is a large chance your pet will "accidentally" get loose or will be put down.

If the pet was the gaslighter's pet before your relationship, you may not be able to take the animal, but you can still report any abuse you witness or suspect. Expect your gaslighter ex to flaunt "custody" of your pet. The ex-wife of one of my clients posted numerous photos on social media of my client's dogs with her new boyfriend.

It's rough, I know, but you have to move on.

Not Sure Whether You Should Leave?

If you're not sure whether you should leave, stop for a minute and think about someone whom you admire. It could be someone in your family, or someone you've never met. What would that person say to you about this situation? What would you say if a friend were in this predicament? Chances are, you'd say *leave*.

Ask yourself what you have learned from this relationship. What are the positives and negatives of this relationship? Where do you see this relationship in a year? In five years? If you can't envision yourself with this person even a year from now, it is time to get out.

Are your needs being met? It may be difficult to remember what your needs even are when you've spent so much time trying to fulfill a gaslighter's needs. Healthy needs in a relationship include:

- Being listened to and heard
- Being yourself without reservation
- Receiving physical affection
- Being safe
- Being respected

How does your relationship fit into your core values? If you've been in a gaslighting relationship for a considerable amount of time, you may not be sure about your values and opinions. This is because the gaslighter has eroded your self-confidence to the point where you aren't sure of what you stand for and what you believe. It is normal to feel lost about these things after being in a relationship with a gaslighter.

A person's values may include:

- Honesty
- Kindness
- Safety and security
- Helping others

What are things your partner ridiculed you about? What are some activities you used to enjoy but were told they were silly or meaningless? Get out there and pick up those activities again. Chances are, you will rediscover yourself quickly if you are engaged in an activity you enjoy.

Are there people in your life from whom you have become distant because of what the gaslighter has told you about them? Would you like to reconnect with them? If so, it may take getting out of your relationship to do so.

Remember that you don't even need a reason to end a relationship. Also give up the idea of having a civil breakup—that is close to impossible with the gaslighter. It will be painful, it will be difficult, but you will be okay. Maybe not right now, maybe not in the immediate future, but you will be okay.

———

NOW LET'S LOOK at how to spot a gaslighter when you are on the dating scene, so you can avoid getting into a relationship with one ever again. Once you become aware of gaslighters' "tells," you are less likely to fall for their manipulation. Gaslighters give away some of their controlling behaviors even before the first date.

3

PASSIONATE, CONFIDENT—
AND OUT FOR CONTROL

How to Avoid Falling for a Gaslighter in the First Place

B EFORE YOU EVEN GET INVOLVED WITH A GASLIGHTER, THERE ARE usually a number of signs you can learn to spot. In fact, signs present in the early stages of dating gaslighters will often tell you everything you need to know about how sticking with them will be detrimental to your well-being.

A few things to know up front: For starters, gaslighters tend to live in larger cities. They need anonymity to succeed at their game. In a big city, it's less likely that word of their bad behavior will get around. And the chances that you'll run into one of their former partners, for example, will decrease as well. Of course, if you live in a city, you aren't going to want to avoid all eligible prospects just because they live in your city, too, but it's one piece of the puzzle that's good to bear in mind.

> "On our second date he talked about how great his former marriage was. I asked him why it ended. He told me it was none of my business. That should have been a clue."
>
> —*Maggie, 27*

"I must be a magnet for manipulators. I guess I'm just too nice, and try to see the good in people. I refuse to get bitter about it. Then they've won."

—*Vanessa, 24*

For some of the same reasons—relative anonymity, unlikelihood that you'll run into an ex—online dating has been a boon for gaslighters. There are other reasons, too, which we'll look at in a moment. I'll also list some first-date red flags and discuss how gaslighters target their victims, whom they see as easy prey, and how not to get romantically involved if your gut tells you something is off.

ONLINE DATING

Apps and websites have become our default mode for dating. We find it easier to meet a potential mate via the Internet rather than the old standbys of friends, bars, social gatherings, and work. It's no surprise why. These days our digital devices are always in our hands. Plus, it's efficient, and in some ways less frightening. You can get a feel for someone before you actually have to talk with the person or interact face to face. However, everything has side effects. The negative side of online dating is that it can make you an easier target for gaslighters (and other creeps).

It's also no surprise that gaslighters like dating apps and websites so much. They can be whomever they want in their profile. They can tell you exactly what you want to hear. Via online dating, gaslighters have access to many people (potential victims) they otherwise wouldn't have met, and they can easily spot clues of vulnerability in people's profiles. Understanding these clues, which we usually give out so unwittingly, is a good first line of defense.

What Makes the Gaslighter Pick You?

Out of all the online dating profiles, what makes a gaslighter contact you? First, lest you think you've been singularly clueless or otherwise to blame, understand that you are rarely the only one. Especially because of the efficiencies of dating apps, gaslighters will usually have many potential targets.

As you learned in Chapter 1, scarcity is a tactic favored by gaslighters, and online dating makes the scarcity game very easy to play. You are chatting back and forth with someone and then—poof!—he disappears. You question what happened. You look up articles to try to figure out whether he is interested. You convince yourself that men are emotional rubber bands—the closer they get, the more they pull back. Just when you are about to give up, the gaslighter shows up again. He has invoked scarcity.

If you respond by playing it cool and acting as if nothing happened, you'll usually pass the "test" and the gaslighter will continue to contact you. If you ask too many questions, such as "Why were you ignoring my messages?" the gaslighter will probably drop you like a hot potato, blame you, and even accuse you of being desperate.

This is because the gaslighter sensed from your response that you would be someone likely to hold him accountable for his behavior in the future, and he doesn't want that! The way things start with someone is usually how they go from that point forward. If you meet someone who doesn't even give an explanation for not contacting you before a first date, how do you think the rest of that relationship is going to work?

The best course of action when encountering someone who "ghosts" and reappears is to not respond and move on.

If your online profile indicates that you:

- Have been single for a while
- Have been married multiple times
- Appear to have money
- Say you see the best in everyone
- Haven't been treated well in the past
- Think your ex was a terrible person
- Want children right away
- Never felt that you "fit in"
- Like taking risks
- Are naughty/bad/wild

. . . . you may as well have painted a bull's-eye on your forehead. These are the very vulnerabilities gaslighters look for. Gaslighters will often rightly assume that if you allude to the things in this list, you are more likely both to get hooked on them and to be more tolerant of their bad behavior.

You may be thinking, *but why would anybody put these things in their profile?* Few people would—in so many words. But we often communicate plenty about ourselves without stating them directly. We say a lot by what we *imply*.

- "I'm ready to be treated well." = "I haven't been treated well in the past."
- "I'm tired of wasting time." = "I'm concerned I won't meet the right person."
- "I see the best in everyone." = "I may accept your lying to me."

So, what should you put in your profile to make yourself more gaslighter-proof? It's a tricky, fine line, but ultimately you want to show that you are active and happy. Gaslighters don't like partners who are positive, upbeat, and independent. They prefer them to be needy, vulnerable, and wounded.

RED FLAGS ON YOUR FIRST DATE

One of the trickiest things about gaslighters is that they are great at hiding their true personality, until you are hooked in. According to Wendy Patrick, JD, PhD, in her article entitled "The Dangerous First Date" in the December 2017 issue of *Psychology Today*, malignant behaviors can masquerade as charming positives in the early stages of dating. For example, protective behavior morphs into pos-

"I knew this date wasn't going to work out, and my date said some things that really offended me. I told him this wasn't going to work, and I was going to leave early. He banged his fist on the table and said I wasn't going to leave yet. That was my cue to get out of there fast."

—Sari, 35

sessiveness; comforting turns into controlling; assertive behavior turns into aggressive behavior; passionate behavior turns violent later on; a direct personality turns into rudeness; and confidence turns into condescension.

"The first things he talked about on our date? His ex-wife and his mother—and not in a pleasant way, either."

—Jessica, 30

Keep an eye out for these behaviors whenever you are on a date. For example, while it may feel comforting, as if you are being taken care of when your date orders your food for you (when you haven't even told him what you want), this is actually a sign of a controlling personality. It feels good at first, but once things start getting real, your partner will be trying to control all your choices in the relationship.

Red flags on a first date with gaslighters include:

- They tell you that you are the most beautiful/wonderful/amazing person they have ever met.
- They talk about long-term commitment with you.
- They talk about having children—not just in general, but with you.
- They talk about themselves . . . . it's almost as if you weren't there.
- They tell you they cheated in a previous relationship.
- They tell you about their dysfunctional family history.
- They don't ask you any questions about your life.
- They don't want to talk about their family.
- They order your food for you.
- They don't use basic manners.
- They treat waitstaff rudely.
- They talk about moving in with you.
- They start holding hands or having other physical contact with you right away.
- They invade your personal space.
- They tell you their previous partner was a "bitch," "asshole," and the like.
- They spend too much time talking about their previous relationships.

- They tell you they have commitment issues, but that they could see committing to you.
- They are vague about what they do for a living.
- Their story doesn't match up with what you read online.
- Their stories aren't consistent.
- They talk about their houses and cars, yet they did not drive their car to your date.
- They dress sloppily.
- They wear clothing that denotes social status (wearing surgical scrubs to dinner, for example. A true surgeon would never do this).
- They name-drop (tell you about well-known people with whom they are friends or colleagues) in a bid to impress you.
- They say they have a well-paying job but ask you to pay for dinner (they will say they forgot their wallet, etc.).
- They talk about travel in other countries that sounds fanciful or unrealistic. (They do this because it is harder to verify.)
- They have excuses for why you couldn't find information on them. (Their identity was stolen, etc.)
- They have difficulty making eye contact.
- They're charming, but it appears not to be genuine.
- They mention how they had a lot of options to choose from but picked you.
- They will not leave when asked.
- They prevent you from leaving.

Again, no one of these items on its own necessarily means you're on a date with a gaslighter, but buyer beware. The signs are usually there.

The Lure of Narcissism

Sometimes gaslighting look an awful lot like narcissism. Narcissistic people tend to look good on paper. They seem too good to be true—because they are. They may be educated, powerful, attractive people—and they also happen to be dangerous manipulators. What appears as confidence, the likes of which you have never seen before, can be intoxicating, until you realize it's part of a pattern—a selfish and endless need for validation.

A History of Cheating

Gaslighters are notorious for being unfaithful in relationships. If someone you are dating tells you she cheated in a previous relationship, pay attention to the red flag. According to a study in 2017 by Kayla Knopp and her colleagues, people who cheated in a previous relationship are three times more likely to report cheating in their current relationship than are people who were faithful in previous relationships.

If you're having a "good date," it can be tempting to think that your date just had a one-off cheating experience and it won't impact you, or she may tell you she's changed, but think again. Cheaters tend to cheat as a pattern of behavior. If you are cheated on, it will affect your future relationships as well. It will sow the seeds of doubt about your potential partner's reliability, if nothing else. In fact, according to Ms. Knopp, people who reported that their previous partner had cheated were four times more likely to be suspicious of their current partner.

Gaslighters Push Alcohol on You

Gaslighters will often order alcohol for you without asking. If you don't order alcohol yourself, gaslighters will cajole and even bully you into ordering a drink. They do this because drinking lowers our inhibitions—and raises the possibility that we'll make poor choices.

It is best to abstain from drinking while on a date with someone new. However, if you do choose to drink, never leave your drink unattended. I'm sure you've heard about people slipping drugs into drinks, and this dramatically increases your chances of being assaulted. Later in this chapter, you'll learn why gaslighters are particularly prone to committing assault.

Gaslighters Don't Do Social Media

Because cheating is so common among gaslighters, avoiding social media is a way to avoid getting caught with someone—or somewhere they aren't supposed to be. If you go on a date and a person tells you he doesn't use Facebook, it could just be that he's not into Facebook. But I suggest following up by asking why. Gaslighters will usually give you a vague answer. If they say, "I'm just not into it" or "I don't have time," take note.

Trust Your Intuition

Most of us get hunches or a "Spidey sense" that something is wrong, and very often these are right on target. If you feel that a situation or person is unsafe to be around, excuse yourself and leave. You don't even have to excuse yourself. Gaslighters sense when people are on to them, and they will switch modes quickly into love-bombing. Gaslighters are masters of pouring it on in the nick of time, getting you to switch from thinking, "This person gives me bad vibes" to "Wow, I really like him." So, get out while you can.

Override the Urge to Be Nice

We, and especially women, are taught from young ages to be caring and polite toward others. It can go against what you believe to stand up to someone and tell him to back off. Remember that the gaslighter does not care about you or your feelings. You are a thing, disposable, a means to an end. It is perfectly acceptable to stand up for yourself and risk being seen as "rude." For example, if you are saying good night to your date at your car and he leans in too close to you, instead of enduring it or trying to wriggle away, say, "No. I need you to back up." If he doesn't move, say it even louder. Remember, with a gaslighter you cannot afford to be concerned with being rude, you have to be concerned with your personal safety.

GASLIGHTERS AND THE RISK OF VIOLENCE

In case you didn't already have enough to worry about, the risks of violence with gaslighters is very real. They are more prone to getting violent because their frustration threshold is so low and they generally don't have good coping skills. You should be prepared to protect yourself. As noted earlier, when you are on a first date with anyone, *never* leave your drink unattended—no matter what. Even if your date tells you there is no need to worry, or that you are being paranoid. If that means you need to take your drink to the bathroom with you, do it. Better yet, refrain from drinking, as we've already discussed. A gaslighter will pressure you to drink so as to make you more vulnerable. A good person will never pressure you to drink.

If your date is pressuring you to drink, he may well be setting you up for assault or rape. I don't have any specific data to support the connection between gaslighting and rape, but since rape is a crime of power and violence, we're wise to include it in this list of cautions.

For information on sexual assault, see Chapter 5 and the Resources section at the end of this book.

WARNING SIGNS IN THE EARLY PHASES OF DATING

So, you've moved beyond the first date and you've begun seeing each other. Here, too, there will usually be all sorts of warning signs. Pay attention to them.

Stay clear if:

- Your family tells you that they think something is "off" with your partner.
- Your partner tells you your family is trying to tear the two of you apart.
- Your partner says you have no right to voice concerns about his or her kids or other family members. For example, you see your partner's kid hit another kid. You tell your partner you are concerned

about his kid's behavior. Your partner tells you that everything is fine and that you didn't see anything of the sort.

- His children and other family members have poor boundaries.
- He overshares or is "enmeshed" with his children and other family members.
- Your partner says he is interested in the same things you are, but when you do those activities together, he is continuously disinterested and bored.
- You are always paying for activities. If you ask your partner to pay, he guilts you into paying. Again.
- Your partner keeps some areas of his life completely separate from you, such as his friends and his phone.

It doesn't matter if your relationship is good 90 percent of the time; if the remaining 10 percent consists of lies and inconsistencies, you need to leave the relationship. Relationships like these only get worse. That 10 percent becomes 20 percent, then 30 percent, and so on. Lies and inconsistencies many times lead to emotional and physical abuse. According to the National Coalition Against Domestic Violence (2017), 10 million people a year are victims of domestic violence. If you are being lied to even just a small part of the time, it's time to look elsewhere.

Quick to Intensity, Slow to Insanity

Wouldn't it be helpful if people could wear big signs stating their pathology when we first meet them? Of course, we don't have this luxury! Also, gaslighters are very good at acting "normal." They make sure you are reeled in before welcoming you into their inner sanctum of insanity. Even mental health professionals have been lured into relationships with gaslighters. They will act so "normal" that even a professional can't always tell who they really are underneath. But that doesn't mean there aren't signs to watch for, as we've seen.

The gaslighter will tend to ramp up the intensity really quickly, while keeping the insanity at bay until you upset him. And then watch out. Upsetting him could be a result of your standing up for yourself, stating something was upsetting to you, or not following some unwritten rule that you didn't know you had to follow. Suddenly, you've gone from queen to crap. The gaslighter sets things up so that you are always going to fall off the pedestal he places you on. By idealizing and then devaluing you, he keeps you off-kilter. This causes you to feel a sense of instability—and that makes you psychologically more dependent on him, which is exactly where he wants you to be.

> "He was the classic 'looks good on paper.' Smart, educated, funny. It wasn't until six months in that I really saw his dark, possessive side."
>
> —Jessie, 28

INFATUATION VERSUS LOVE

As we saw in Chapter 2, gaslighters love to "love-bomb" in the beginning of a relationship. They put you up on a pedestal. They shower you with attention. Keep in mind that gaslighters try to get you to fall for an idea of who they are, not their actual person. The real person is behind a mask. Gaslighters know how to act like a "regular" person to get you ensnared.

You may feel an instant sense of "love" for this person. But no one falls in love that quickly. What you are probably feeling is infatuation. You're on cloud nine, your heart races when you see the person, and you want to get naked every time you are in proximity. It feels amazing! But infatuation is also tenuous. There is no real sense of permanency. You feel insecure. You feel as if you may lose this person. You feel jealous when she is going out with her friends. You want to spend all your time with this person, and being apart from her causes you distress.

Love is a deeper feeling. Sometimes people experience infatuation in the beginning of their relationship, and it fades within about six months to two years. This is when things start getting real. Some relationships end at this point because things just aren't exciting enough once the butterflies and excitement wear off. This is also when you might start seeing a gaslighter's true self. In a healthy relationship, the early stages are exciting, but there is also a sense of calm and connection. The physical connection is great, and the emotional connection makes the physical even better. When you love someone, you enjoy being with her, and are also good with having your own interests and some alone time. In a healthy relationship, your partner is okay with you going out with your friends—in fact, a healthy partner encourages you to go out, and makes a point to get to know your friends.

Keep in mind the difference between infatuation and love when you are dating. Tell your brain to slow down a little so you can think more rationally about who you're "falling in love" with. With gaslighters, things usually don't go from infatuation to love, they go from infatuation to misery. While I don't want to take all the fun out of infatuation, it's so important not to mistake it for love—and to be on the lookout for the signs of gaslighting and manipulation.

SWINDLING AND CONNING

Beyond control, gaslighters often have other motives and objectives. Some gaslighters' main objective is to con you out of money, cars, and property. They specifically target people in online dating sites because they are seen as "easy marks." These gaslighters tend to target older and wealthier men and women. What starts out as "I forgot my wallet at home" on a date turns into you signing over your possessions and other assets to him.

"He told me he was a doctor. It turns out he was a drug addict who hid it very well. He started asking me for money and tried to forge my name on prescriptions."

—Jane, 68

Case Study: John Meehan (based on reporting by the *Los Angeles Times* 10/1/17–10/8/17)

The story of John Meehan is one that seems like a made-for-TV movie, but it really happened, as was reported in a series in the *Los Angeles Times* and in a podcast by Christopher Goffard (2017). Meehan was a man whose life revolved around conning people, specifically women. He consistently lied to women, stating that he was, among other things, an anesthesiologist who had volunteered in Iraq with Doctors Without Borders. John forbade his first wife from contacting his family. When she went against his wishes, he exploded with anger. His wife had discovered that John was not who he claimed to be. John threatened her repeatedly, bragging about his mob ties. In 2014, he found Debra Newell, a successful business owner, on an online dating site. John also told Debra he was an anesthesiologist who had spent time in Iraq with Doctors Without Borders. He pushed quickly for them to get married, tying the knot just months after they started dating.

Debra's family were the ones who uncovered John's lies. He was a nurse who had lost his nursing license and served prison time for possession of narcotics. Confronted by these lies, John lashed out. Debra left him. John then begged for forgiveness, telling her it was a misunderstanding, and her family didn't want her to find love and be happy. She went back to him. When she left a second time, John threatened her and her family. He told Debra that she had taken money from him, when in fact she had given him money. He sent nude photos of her to her family. Finally, he stalked and then attacked Debra's daughter, Terra, stabbing her repeatedly. She grabbed his knife and stabbed him in self-defense. Terra survived; John died of his wounds.

Why would a successful woman like Debra fall prey to a con artist like John Meehan? Wouldn't she have picked up on the signs that John was gaslighting her? Not necessarily. Gaslighters are very, very good at acting like regular people. They almost "overdo" the acting normal bit, and seem too good to be true. John knew what a successful woman like Debra would want—a stable, "together," cultured person. And John knew how to deliver with the lies.

Add the fact that Debra's sister had been shot and killed by her husband, and Debra's mother testified *for* her daughter's killer—which led to him getting a lighter sentence. What did this model for Debra? That men are in the right, no matter the degree of their heinous behavior? Sadly, it would seem so. Your family history has quite a bit to do with whether you are prey to a gaslighter. You'll learn more about families and gaslighting in Chapter 6.

PROTECTING YOURSELF

"From now on I'm doing a background check on my dates. A friend told me I was being dramatic, but I'd really like to know ahead of time if he has a history of domestic violence or any other violent behavior."

—June, 27

As you've seen so far, we need to be on alert while out on a date or searching online for one. Never let down your guard. Know that there are gaslighters out there whose main objective is to find prey. Follow these tips to protect yourself:

- If you are considering online dating, choose a paid site or app rather than a free one. Gaslighters can be notoriously cheap, so using a paid site may narrow your chances of connecting with one.
- Have your friends review your online dating profile and photo before you post them. Ask your most cautious friends to do this, as they are more likely to point out anything that might signal that you're red meat for the hungry gaslighter.
- Try meeting people in face-to-face get-togethers instead of online or, once you do meet online and start chatting, arrange a face-to-face meeting so you can be a better judge.
- Date people who have been recommended to you by your friends. It's even better if your friend has known the person for a considerable amount of time—since childhood, for example.
- Do a background check before making another date. See the Resources section at the end of this book for suitable services.
- Google the person before you go out with him. If there are any inconsistencies between the information you see online and what the person has told you in his profile or from chatting with him, simply stop all communication. That's a big red flag.
- Before you go out on a date, arrange with friends to have an SOS message you can send to them, so that they can then call you and

say there is an emergency and you need to leave. Do not accept the gaslighter's offer to drive you.

- Do not get in the gaslighter's car. Part of a gaslighter's MO (standard mode of operating) is to get you on their territory and isolate you. Once you are removed from your original location, your chances of being assaulted or killed increase dramatically.
- Do not bring the gaslighter back to your home, or go to his, on the first date.
- Do not exchange any racy photos before meeting this person.
- Arrange to meet in a public location.
- If something seems off in your online communication with a date, cease talking with him. While "ghosting" or just disappearing on someone is not recommended in healthy dating relationships, you must "ghost" a gaslighter. To continue contact, even to say "We're not a good fit," makes you more likely to be manipulated by him.
- If you need to end contact with the person, block all phone numbers, e-mails, and profiles associated with him.
- Report the person to the online dating site if he has violated any of the terms of the site, such as harassment, slurs, or stalking.

> "He told me he was a surgeon. But there was no record of him in the state health department license lookup. He told me that he had just moved to the state so his license wouldn't show up yet. He teased me about being 'paranoid' and 'watching too many cop shows.' It turns out he wasn't a doctor at all."
>
> —*Janis, 55*

- Contact law enforcement if you have been threatened, harassed, or stalked—online or in "real life." Seek a restraining order from the court. See the Resources section at the end of this book for more information on restraining orders.
- Do not post warnings about a gaslighter on websites. The gaslighter can easily trace these posts back to you.
- Trust your gut. Even if your friends tell you what a great person he or she is, but you still feel uneasy about it, do not go out with the person again.

MAKE A LIST OF WHAT YOU ARE
LOOKING FOR IN A PARTNER

It may not sound very exciting, but when it comes to dating, it's always best to make choices with our head instead of our heart. When we are infatuated with someone, we tend to look past warning signs. Our brain goes into a temporary state of insanity. We lose reason. "Oh, you're an ax murderer? I can totally work with that." To prepare yourself to make a healthy choice, try this exercise. Sit down and make a list of the qualities of your ideal partner. Get as specific as possible. Items you may want to include:

- Likes dogs / cats
- Family gets along
- Listens
- Wants to work out conflict
- Exercises regularly
- Has a stable job
- Speaks respectfully to me and others

Focus on positive attributes. Instead of "doesn't call people names," try using "speaks respectfully to people" instead. This helps you focus more on what you want rather than what you don't want.

When you have met someone that you think is just the best thing ever, take a look at your list. How many of your desired qualities does this person have? Looking at this list helps you use your brain to make a wise dating decision, when your heart wants to go solely on emotions.

TRUST THE SIGNS, USE THOSE SMARTS!

I trust that this has all been helpful. Dating in general is fraught with risk because gaslighters can be so clever, so charming, and so seemingly "normal." And online dating can make you easy prey for gaslighters. But now you know the red flags. You've got some new tools to protect yourself in the dating world. If I had to pick one piece of advice on dating, it's this: trust the signs. As Maya Angelou said, "When someone shows you who they are, believe them the first time."

———

NOW, LET'S TURN to another arena where gaslighters often do their best work: the workplace. We'll look at how to work with people who don't have your best interests in mind, how to report gaslighting behavior in the most effective ways, and how to find the laws than can protect you from harassment.

4

SABOTEURS, HARASSERS, OFF-LOADERS, AND THUNDER STEALERS

Gaslighters in the Workplace

ATTHEW THOUGHT HE LANDED HIS DREAM JOB RIGHT OUT OF UNIversity. He was working for a large firm in the city. As a new hire, he was expected to take on a large amount of assignments and work longer hours than his coworkers. He had a direct supervisor, with whom he had initially interviewed for the position. From the beginning, Matthew had the feeling that the supervisor didn't care for him. However, this was a great job opportunity and Matthew thought the supervisor would be fine over time—he had never had an issue working for someone before. One thing Matthew noticed from the beginning was his supervisor's facial expressions—he looked at Matthew with an expression of utter contempt. Matthew wrote it off to, "Maybe he looks at everyone that way." Matthew would turn in assignments as required, but his supervisor would inevitably tell him that he never received the assignment. Matthew noticed his supervisor gave him a great deal more assignments than other new hires in his same position. The entrance code was changed on the office door and everyone was given the new code except Matthew—he was routinely left off of interoffice emails. Matthew asked the supervisor to make sure he received these emails, but the supervisor said Matthew's email address was included on all the emails, and that it was Matthew's responsibility to make sure he received the information. The supervisor would also walk by Matthew's desk and mutter insults to him, without making eye contact. One day the supervisor muttered a comment about Matthew's sexual orientation. Matthew decided enough was enough. He went to talk to the supervisor and told him he was aware that he was using abusive language towards him. The supervisor responded, "What on earth are you talking about?" Matthew thought that maybe the supervisor was right—maybe he hadn't really heard his supervisor say those things. When it was time for Matthew's work performance review, the supervisor had written, "sub-par in attitude and completion of tasks". This was a blatant lie. When Matthew refused to sign the performance review, the supervisor threatened to fire him. Matthew got on well with his coworkers—he couldn't figure out why his supervisor appeared to target and sabotage him. Matthew started blaming himself. Finally, a friend told him that it most definitely was not Matthew's fault—his supervisor was a gaslighter. Gaslighters don't just wreak havoc in our personal lives. They have destroyed many careers and companies. They manipulate coworkers and subordinates into doing work for them, then take credit. They make false claims of harassment when they, in fact, are the harassers. (Actually, I think it's safe to say that most, if not all, harassment is a form of gaslighting.) They throw coworkers under the bus. They refuse to take any responsibility for their behavior. It is one thing to mess with your personal life—it is quite another to encounter someone hell bent on taking down your professional life.

In a survey of UK workplaces, 35% of women said they had experienced sexual harassment while working. Of women under the age of 30, 62% had experienced sexual harassment in the workplace. Unwanted touching, hugging, and kissing was experienced by 14% of women while at work (Savage, 2018). In the US, several women have alleged that Hollywood producer Harvey Weinstein threatened, and in some cases ended, their career when they refused to have sexual contact with him. He was a classic workplace gaslighter. And he's not the only recent example; numerous other celebrities and public figures are facing allegations of workplace harassment. In this chapter, you will learn how to iden-

> "My coworker would be on-call but would refuse to answer the phone. This meant clients would call me instead. I talked to higher-ups about it, but he had some damaging info on the boss, so he got away with it."
>
> —Juan, 40

tify a workplace gaslighter, protect yourself and your career, and figure out ways to avoid ever working with a gaslighter again. You'll also read more about gaslighting and sexual harassment, abuse, and violence in Chapter 5.

How do you know you work with a gaslighter? You may witness the following behaviors:

- Takes credit for your hard work.
- Gives you backhanded compliments.
- Ridicules you in front of your coworkers.
- Blames everything on you.
- Knows your weak spot and exploits it.
- Actively tries to get you demoted or fired.
- Lies to get ahead.
- Seems to compete with everyone to be "the best" at work.
- Spreads gossip about you, and denies doing it when you confront her.
- Sabotages your work.
- Gives you the wrong times and dates for important meetings.
- Pressures you to do something unethical.
- Is jealous of your accomplishments instead of congratulating you.
- Shows displays of anger when things don't go her way.
- Bullies and threaten you and others.
- Sexually harasses you and others.

Gaslighters can make even the least stressful of jobs into a complete nightmare. Their scheming, sabotaging, and one-upping never seem

"It didn't matter what the project was about—this guy would take credit for everything. Not only that, he would tell the boss that we were slackers and he had to make up for our incompetence. He went the extra mile."

—Doug, 55

to stop. When they are caught in disrespectful or harmful behavior by an employer, gaslighters seem to double down and actually increase their maladaptive behavior. Some may calm the storm for just a brief period of time before resuming their gaslighting ways. Very rarely do gaslighters stop their manipulative behaviors. As you read earlier in the book, many gaslighters are so lacking in self-awareness that they don't see their bad behavior. They truly believe that everyone else has the problem, not them.

SEXUAL AND OTHER HARASSMENT IN THE WORKPLACE

"My coworker would brush his hand against my butt as he walked by, and say 'excuse me' like it was an accident. He was really slick when he did it, so no one saw it. I was going to report it, but I was concerned he would just say I was lying. What proof did I have?"

—Lydia, 28

Gaslighters use harassment as a way to gain control over you and over their workplace. They're betting that by harassing you, you will stay quiet about the other bad behaviors they're engaging in at work.

One type of harassment is sexual harassment. Sexual harassment is against the law according to the Equality Act 2010.

You may be the victim of sexual harassment if:

- You are told your job or an assignment depends on sexual activity.
- You receive unwelcome sexual advances.
- A person touches you without your consent.
- Someone is standing too close.
- A person or persons displays offensive material.
- You are asked for sexual favors.
- Workplace decisions are made on the basis of sexual advances being accepted or rejected.

Other forms of harassment include:

- Employees playing "pranks" on you.
- Your items are continually removed and then replaced on your desk.
- Employees tamper with your food in the office refrigerator.
- Your locker is broken into.
- Having your personal items hidden from you.
- Unauthorized employees entering your workspace without permission.

While most gaslighters don't take their workplace behavior to the level where it qualifies legally as harassment, some do, and this is especially true when you are working in an environment that appears to reward bad behavior. For example, while there's nothing wrong, at least on the face of it, with an employer's use of incentives to increase productivity, this provides a perfect setup for gaslighters. They'll do whatever they feel is necessary to gain an advantage over others, and this includes devious and damaging behavior. In some areas of the business world, being ruthless earns a gaslighter respect, but this is really nothing more than fear of the gaslighter disguised as respect. In this section, we'll take a look at where aggressive work habits actually constitute harassment, and the steps you can take to fight it.

"I had a boss that would stand and watch me as I worked. This wasn't just watching—it was leering. It was really creepy. Towards the end of the day when there were less people in the office, I started feeling unsafe and would bolt out of there."

—Marisol, 36

Harassment is about power. It is about "keeping you in your place." Gaslighters love to hold power over people's heads. They especially thrive off knowing that your livelihood—your work—hangs in the balance.

Gaslighters can be very subtle in their harassment—just enough to get to you but not quite enough to prove. Many harassment cases end up coming down to a "he said, she said" situation, one person's word against the other. For that reason, and concerns about retaliation, many cases of harassment have never even been filed, let alone resolved.

Also, when you first encounter harassment, it is very common to feel so in shock that you doubt yourself or your perception of the experience. *Did he really just say what I thought he said? Maybe he didn't mean it the way it came across.* If you have lived with a gaslighter, and particularly if you were raised by one, you will be even more likely to question your sense of reality. You were trained early on to disbelieve your own eyes and ears, so of course you automatically question your experience. Believe what you are seeing and hearing, even if a gaslighter tells you otherwise.

EQUALITY ACT 2010

Harassment is unlawful under the Equality Act 2010. Harassment is defined as: *Unwanted conduct related to a relevant protected characteristic, which has the purpose or effect of violating an individual's dignity or creating an intimidating, hostile, degrading, humiliating or offensive environment for that individual* (Acas, 2014).

Bullying is defined as: *Offensive, intimidating, malicious, or insulting behaviour, an abuse or misuse of power through means that undermine, humiliate, denigrate, or injure the recipient* (Acas, 2014).

Bullying or harassment may be an individual acting against an individual, or it may involve groups of people. Bullying or harassment can be overt (clear) or covert (hidden). Either way, it is against the law. Examples of bullying or harassing behavior include:

- Spreading malicious rumors.
- Unfair treatment.
- Picking on or undermining an employee through constant criticism or overloading with work.
- Denying an employee training or promotion opportunities.
- Overbearing supervision or other misuse of power or position.
- Unwelcome sexual advances.

Bullying and harassment can occur face-to-face, by email, by letter, or by phone. While bullying itself isn't against the law in the UK, harassment is. Harassment is defined as when the unwanted behavior is related to any one of the following:

- Age
- Gender (including gender reassignment)
- Disability
- Religion or belief
- Marital status or civil partnership
- Pregnancy or maternity—including breastfeeding
- Race
- Sexual orientation

Steps You Can Take

The UK government recommends sorting out the problem informally at first. Consider contacting the gaslighter directly about his behavior. You have the option of doing this in person, or in writing. If it is in person, consider having a witness present. As you have learned, gaslighters are very adept at twisting the truth. What happened between you and the gaslighter will certainly not be the story the gaslighter reports to others. Having a witness backs up your version of events.

"My coworker would call me racial slurs, and would do it with a smile and in a sweet tone of voice. It still gives me chills thinking about it. I told him to stop, and he kept going. I even told my boss. Nothing happened. I didn't know what to do next. I was worried about losing my job if I pushed it further."

—*Dan, 35*

Contacting the gaslighter through writing is a way to create a paper or electronic trail. It is difficult for the gaslighter to lie about what you said when it is right there in an e-mail. While confronting the gaslighter may be very uncomfortable for you, it puts the gaslighter on notice and will help you build a case if the harassment continues. If this is not

"I co-owned a business with a guy that was a total gaslighter. He told our customers that I was 'mentally unstable' and to just come to him for their accounts. Finally, one of the customers said to me, 'I get the feeling you don't know about this . . . .' and told me the whole story. I sold my part of the business and got out."

—*Wade, 60*

possible, or you are concerned for your safety, the government recommends you speak to your manager, human resources department, or union representative.

If you still have not received relief from the gaslighter's harassment, you can make a formal complaint using your employer's grievance procedure. If you are still being harassed after taking this step, you can take legal action at an employment tribunal. If you make a claim to an employment tribunal, they expect you to have tried to resolve the issue with your employer.

You can also call the Advisory, Conciliation, and Arbitration Service (Acas) for advice. Contact information for Acas can be found in the Resources at the end of this book.

GASLIGHTERS AS SUPERVISORS

Gaslighting is not just the behavior of employees. Plenty of people in powerful positions are gaslighters, too. You may have a supervisor who gaslights you. Gaslighters know how to manipulate and work the system. They ride to the top by lying about their accomplishments, and they succeed on other people's hard work. They may have even blackmailed a person or persons to get promoted. They are also more likely to use sexual favors for promotions. Gaslighters can also be good at a job as other people can. This may be one of the most frustrating parts of having a gaslighter boss—they are actually competent at what they do, making it more difficult to get them fired.

Here are some signs to watch out for.

They Will Watch You as You Work

Supervisors who observe you as you work is nothing new, but gaslighters will do it to extremes and in unsavory ways. You may find that your gaslighting supervisor watches you much more than he does your co-workers. You may also find that he hangs around you a little too closely when there are fewer employees around. He may even try to isolate you from your peers.

This "watching" crosses into leering—looking at you in a way that makes you feel uncomfortable. You have the right to say loudly, "Please step back." This makes it known to others in the office that this person is behaving inappropriately—and it also creates witnesses. Gaslighters will back off if they know others may see them as less than perfect. Their image is everything.

Gaslighting Supervisors Can Gang Up

Gaslighters will sometimes band together and gang up on you. Even people who aren't typically gaslighters will join in. This is known as "crowd psychology." We are more likely to engage in a behavior when others are—even if it is against our beliefs. Group behavior is contagious and can make us feel less responsible for our actions. An employer may also put pressure on supervisors to gaslight employees.

"My supervisors got together and gaslighted me as a group. They all made up false information about my job performance in a quest to get me fired."

—Jameel, 28

They Review You Poorly, Despite the Evidence

If your gaslighting boss calls you into a performance review meeting, have another supervisor in the room as a witness. If you have an unfavorable and unwarranted evaluation, you can request another performance evaluation from a higher-level supervisor. If asked why, you

"I loved my job—and I was good at it. But I didn't count on an effort by my bosses to get me fired. They were setting up situations where it looked like I wasn't doing my job. Like they would tell the higher-ups that I refused to work on something, and they had never even talked to me about it. I was starting to wonder if they had asked me and I just forgot. But then I started writing down exactly what they said to me. They were just lying. I had enough one day and walked out. Not one of my bosses was willing to 'break ranks' and say enough is enough."

—Amber, 28

can just say that you noticed some discrepancies between your work and the evaluation you received. Make sure you show up to the evaluation with documentation of your accomplishments at work. You need to have concrete evidence why the performance evaluation you received was not accurate. Also review your employee manual to see whether there are specific steps your company requires when you feel a performance review is not accurate.

If your gaslighting boss tells you that you need to sign your performance evaluation and you believe the evaluation is damaging or incorrect, you are under no obligation to sign. Performance reviews are company policy, not law. Usually signing the performance review means that you just agree that you received it. However, if you see fine print that says "I agree to the comments and evaluation above," do not sign it. Your performance evaluation may have a comment box on it. I strongly recommend against leaving written comments on your own evaluation, especially on the spot. Think about what you want to write first. This prevents you from writing something from your emotions rather than from facts. You can send in your comments later.

HARASSMENT AT A UNIVERSITY

"I went to my professor's office about needing to raise my grade, and he told me that maybe I could help him out too. I told him no way. He said that if I ever said anything, we could both be in trouble."

—Casey, 22

Gaslighting goes on in school and university settings just like anywhere else. Professors and teaching assistants can gaslight students or lower-level faculty; students can even gaslight their professors. Remember, gaslighters feed off being in power. If a student earns a C in your class, and you won't change it to an A, she can tell the department that you stalked her. That's a form of gaslighting, too.

If you are either a student or an employee at your university and are being harassed, or you know someone who is, you have options. See your student or employee handbook for grievance procedures. Many campuses have an advisor, faculty advocate, or a student welfare department. In addition, you always have the option of calling the police if you have been threatened or harassed.

Don't accept "We'll talk to him" or "Are you sure you just didn't misunderstand?" as sufficient responses from your university. You need to see proof that steps have been taken to make sure this behavior

> "The TA (teaching assistant) hit on me, and I turned him down. After that he would always ask me the hardest questions in class. He also recorded me as absent when I was in class."
>
> —Reese, 23

doesn't happen to you or any other student in the future. It is in your best interest to retain an attorney. While many universities take swift action in reports of abuse, there have been major discrepancies in the ways UK universities record harassment and assault, with 213 incidents in the past seven years where the alleged perpetrator's identity wasn't recorded (Batty and Cherubini, 2018). Make your voice heard and hold others accountable.

HARASSMENT BY CLIENTS

It's not just employers and coworkers that can gaslight you; your clients can, too. It can be a real conundrum for professionals when a person who has hired you for help turns on you. Most often such individuals

> "My client didn't want to pay his bill, so he reported me to the Bar for 'misconduct.'"
>
> —James, 48

turn on you because you have told them something that they didn't want to hear, or they owe you money.

Even though you may have confidentiality rules in your profession, this does not mean you aren't protected from threatening behavior. Once your client has reported you to a professional board, they have chosen to break confidentiality. You also have the right to contact the police and provide a client's name if he has threatened you.

If you are a mental health professional, one way to reduce bogus complaints from gaslighters is to have your clients pay their full copay or session fee before they can make another appointment. When a gaslighting client owes you money, and it has been adding up, he will try what-

"A client would order something, then tell my supervisor I didn't fill the order properly and was rude to her. I see no other reason she did it besides to get a kick out of causing drama."

—Ken, 36

ever it takes to get out of paying. As you've read before, gaslighters like to look as if they have money when they often do not, whether because they have trouble keeping a job or are just very tight with their money (which gaslighters notoriously are).

You may also consider stating in your consent form that if a client has an issue with you, you would like him to come talk to you first. If his concern has not been resolved to his satisfaction, he can then report it to your licensing board or credentialing organization. Provide this contact information in your consent form. Sometimes being transparent about the grievance process reduces complaints.

Your professional organization may be able to refer you to an attorney for pro bono (free) legal advice. Your licensing board or bar may also have information on your rights when a client harasses you. For more information on your rights as a professional, see the Resources at the end of this book.

GASLIGHTERS AND WORKPLACE VIOLENCE

"My coworker would make comments about wishing we were dead, but would always add he was joking. He would accuse us of being too sensitive when we complained."

—Claire, 32

While gaslighters tend to try to keep as perfect an image as possible, they also may be more prone to violence due to their tendency to personalize other people's behavior. When gaslighters "personalize," they take someone's behavior toward them as a personal attack. In other words, if you criticize a gaslighter's work, she'll feel that her ego has been attacked. Being fired from a job, to a gaslighter, is a personal affront, and there must be retaliation against the employer.

Workplace violence can refer to any of the following behaviors:

- Damage to property or sabotage of electronic information
- Stalking
- Threats of violence
- Body-to-body combat (punching, kicking)
- The use of weapons (guns, knives, etc.; arson, or bomb threats)

How can you prevent or protect yourself from a gaslighter who may engage in workplace violence?

- Report disturbing employee behavior to your employer.
- Have a protocol established in the event of workplace violence.
- Run drills for the event of workplace violence.
- Have a meeting place if you need to evacuate the building.

You have the right to always feel safe at your workplace.

While firearms and weapons attacks in the UK are very rare, the National Police Chiefs' Council (NPCC) recommends the following steps:

Run
- Leave your belongings behind.
- Insist that others come with you, but don't let their indecision slow you down.
- Once you've identified a safe route, run.
- If you can't find a safe route, hide.

Hide
- Consider your exits and escape routes when finding a hiding place. Avoid dead-ends and bottlenecks.
- Try to find places with reinforced walls.
- Lock yourself in a room and move away from the door.

- Be as quiet as possible—switch your mobile phone to silent and switch off vibrate.
- Don't shout for help or do anything that will give away your hiding place.

Tell

- If you're able to evacuate, get as far away from the danger area as possible.
- Try to stop others from entering, as long as this won't put you in danger.
- Dial 999 and tell them clearly the location of you and the attackers.

Follow Police Instructions

- When the police arrive, they may not be able to distinguish you from the attackers. They may be very firm with you—do everything the police tell you, and do not make any sudden movements or gestures that may be perceived as a threat. Stay calm and do not wave your arms or shout. Keep your hands visible at all times so the police know that you are not armed.

In summary, when faced with a firearms or weapons attack at your workplace, follow these steps: run, hide, tell.

Gaslighters may have a history of law-breaking, use of lethal weapons, abusive behavior, causing fear in others, vindictiveness, stalking, threatening family members of a victim, and a disregard for human life, even before they tip into physical assault.

HOW ELSE TO PROTECT YOURSELF

Besides filing a harassment claim, if you work with or for a gaslighter, here are some steps you can take to protect yourself from your colleague's undermining and sometimes illegal behavior:

Never Be Alone with a Workplace Gaslighter

Always have someone else in the room when you are meeting with a gaslighter. If you cannot find a witness before a meeting, reschedule it. You may feel you are putting your career in jeopardy by rescheduling an important meeting, but your career depends on you not being alone with this person. If a gaslighter

> "My supervisor would ask me to meet her in her office for meetings. Due to her past behavior, I told her I would feel more comfortable if someone were present. She became irate and threatened to fire me."
>
> —*Michael, 38*

follows you into an area where others are not present, leave the space or insist on bringing a coworker in with you. Without witnesses, you are more likely to be sexually harassed, touched inappropriately, or abused. The gaslighter will also lie about what interaction the two of you had. With a witness, gaslighters are more likely to behave appropriately. This is especially true if gaslighters know the witness hasn't caught on to who they really are. Gaslighters are still invested in the witness wanting to idealize them. If you're alone with a gaslighter and file a complaint about her, the gaslighter will just tell people that you are crazy, or you were hitting on them. As you read earlier in the book, gaslighters know one of the most effective ways to dismiss you is by calling you crazy.

Meet with Your Boss Once a Week

Have a weekly meeting with your boss so you can review projects you are working on, and also update your boss with your progress. Track everything in writing. This way, if a gaslighter claims the work was all hers, you have previous notifications to your boss that the work was truly yours. Meeting with

> "My coworker tried to take credit for my project – she did this often, taking credit for others' work. Luckily, because I had met with my supervisor every week, he knew that I had completed this project 100 percent on my own. The next week she was sacked."
>
> —*Karen, 44*

your boss on a weekly basis also gives you a chance to air grievances as they happen.

If your boss says he doesn't believe the gaslighter would do something like this, document that – include the date and time and content of his response.

If your boss says you need to work it out with your coworker first, tell him you've tried and found the other person volatile, and that trying to work things out seems like it would make it worse. Show him your documentation of what the gaslighter has been doing.

If your gaslighter is the boss, or if you have no superiors or human resources department to turn to, seek legal advice or contact Acas. For information on legal services and Acas, see the Resources at the end of this book.

At the very least, ask to move to a different cubicle or office, as far away from the gaslighter as possible.

Do Not Drink at Office Parties

At office parties and other social events related to work, refrain from drinking. Getting even a little bit sloppy will give a gaslighter prime opportunities to victimize you, whether it is by stealing from you, lying about your behavior, or even assaulting you. If you feel you need a drink in your hand to "blend" at the party, get a seltzer water with lime. It looks like a gin and tonic, and no one will be the wiser. If someone does ask you why you're not drinking, say you're the designated driver or that you are taking antibiotics and can't drink. Better yet, say you just don't feel like it.

> "I drank too much at an office party, and my coworker said I made a pass at her. I did nothing of the sort. I have witnesses, but she continues her lies. She's always wanted to get me fired."
>
> —Ken, 36

Another reason not to drink at the office party is that you may be more tempted or likely to tell the gaslighter off—and this will not end well for you. Remember this. You will never win a fight with gaslighters. They welcome fights—they feed off the energy. Also, if gaslighters make up a story about your "outrageous" behavior toward them at an office party, if you have been drinking it unfortunately adds credibility to their lies.

Document, Document, Document

Keep notes about your interaction with gaslighters. As you read earlier in this chapter, documentation is essential if you need to report their behavior to your employer or the EEOC. If you consult an attorney, you will be asked for documentation. In your documentation, include:

- Date of the event
- Time of the event
- Who was present
- What was said (use direct quotes as much as possible)
- What behaviors occurred

Keep this information on a personal device, rather than a work-issued one. If you are fired from your job, your device will be taken from you, and now your employer has your documentation. Do not discuss gaslighters' behavior with others via texts on a work-issued phone, or via workplace e-mail. In addition, keep this documentation password-protected.

Find Employment Elsewhere

One of the most effective ways of distancing yourself from a workplace gaslighter is to change jobs. You may need to leave your employer or, depending on your type of work and size of company, you may be able to transfer to another department or job site or location within the company. While this is not the easiest solution, it gets you away from the root of the problem. If you have brought your concerns to your employer and it doesn't appear that the gaslighter will be demoted or terminated, consider leaving. While this is far from fair, keep in mind that gaslighters continue ramping up their behavior. In other words, it will only get worse.

You may feel that by your quitting or changing your job, a gaslighter has "won". However, this is not the case. You have won, because you have removed yourself from a toxic environment. A gaslighter in the office can be a result of a system-wide problem. If you followed the company's guidelines for reporting unwanted behavior and the gaslighter is still working there, that might be proof enough that you work in a toxic work environment. Better to get out than to continue to suffer.

If you are unsure if your rights have been violated, consult with an attorney who specializes in labour law. An attorney can tell you what your workplace rights are and if your experience violates any laws. For more information on your workplace rights, see the Resources at the end of this chapter.

If You Are an Employer

If you are an employer, check in with your employees on a regular basis. Have a written code of conduct and standard operating procedures (SOPs) regarding harassment in the workplace. Your SOPs should include the steps an employee should take to report harassment, as well as a clear guarantee that there will be no retaliation. Your investigation of a harassment claim should be done immediately after a complaint is filed and completed in an unbiased way. For more information on how you can protect your company and your employees from harassment and establish guidelines in cases of harassment, see the Resources in the back of this book.

—

IN THIS CHAPTER, we've looked at how gaslighters target others in the workplace, including issues of sexual harassment. In the next chapter, we'll take a closer look at this and also how gaslighting is often a part of violence and domestic abuse.

5

YOU, TOO

Sexual Harassment, Violence, Domestic Abuse, and Gaslighters

M ORE ATTENTION HAS BEEN DRAWN TO SEXUAL HARASSMENT RE-cently, and that in turn has drawn more attention to domestic violence. Gaslighters are perpetrators of both. Manipulation and control are a way of life for gaslighters, and they try to take everyone down with them. Whether you are experiencing harassment at work, home, or in dating, it is a very real (and continuing phenomenon) that has resulted in victims being questioned as to whether they were really harassed, and also being discredited for speaking out. Domestic violence perpetrators use gaslighting as a way to convince their victims that they are crazy, and no one will believe them if they report that they are being abused. This continues a cycle of escalating abuse that sometimes leads to death.

#METOO

Although the #MeToo hashtag phenomenon began in 2017 on social media due to allegations against movie producer Harvey Weinstein, the actual Me Too movement was started by Tarana Burke in 2005. Harassment by gaslighters has been occurring for a very long time, with women the usual target. The disclosures of Weinstein's alleged abuse have made it safer for other women to come forward and disclose sometimes years of abuse they suffered by Weinstein and other gaslighters. In the case of Weinstein, these allegations went back three decades, including to a settlement in 1990, yet just now, in 2017, were these stories fulling coming to light.

Why don't victims come forward earlier? Gaslighters who harass others tend to have quite a bit of power. When victims have come forward, they have been told they will be ruining their career, their family, and/or their reputation by coming forward. They have even been threatened with harm, and their families threatened with harm. And there is the classic "No one will believe you anyway."

While we don't yet know whether there has been an overall decrease in harassment since 2017's #MeToo movement, we do know that more victims are speaking out. Women (and men) have endured harassment for many years, and many victims still do not feel comfortable disclosing their abuse.

We have reached the point in society where it is safer to come out into the light and speak your truth than stay quiet and ashamed for something that is not your fault. However, we still have a long way to go. Speaking out about it is a huge step, but now we need to put into place both parameters to reduce and hopefully eliminate harassment, and measures to provide serious consequences to those that do harass.

We also need to have a clear definition of harassment. You or someone you know may have been told that it wasn't harassment because you had flirted with that person previously. Or if drinking or drug use is involved, that you "set yourself up" to be harassed or abused. Let me make this very clear: No one "asks" to be harassed or abused. If you are not conscious, you cannot give consent, no matter what a gaslighter may tell you.

Companies, throughout history, have tended to protect themselves rather than coming out against a harasser. Take for instance, Matt Lauer's firing from NBC's *Today Show*. NBC stated that it had no idea that Lauer was allegedly harassing women in the workplace until a colleague came forward. A *Vanity Fair* article by Sarah Ellison (2017) alleges that Lauer targeted women that were interns, pages, and production assistants—women with less power than he had at NBC. Younger, new employees are targets for gaslighters, as many are starting out at their first job, and getting fired for reporting harassment, or being told that they will never work in the field again if they report harassment, is a very real fear. Further, former employees also claimed in a *Variety* article (Setoodeh and Wagmeister 2017) that Lauer had a button under the desk in his office, so he could lock the door inside.

If these allegations are true then it shows how a gaslighter can wield their power as a weapon to keep victims in their control. They analyze and stalk people like a predator and prey. First, everyone is a potential victim. This can't be stated enough. However, a person who has free will is of no interest to them. Gaslighters home in on people they sense have vulnerabilities that can be exploited. They know that if you are new to the field and this is your first job, or that they can control your rise in a field where they hold importance, you are less likely to fight their harassment. Their telling you that if you reject their harassment or discuss their behavior with others, you will lose your job and all your prospects in your chosen field, carries a tremendous amount of weight to someone who needs that job. This buys them submission and silence. But now, victims realize there is safety in numbers and are speaking out.

It does appear that more companies are realizing the legal ramifications of not addressing harassment claims immediately. Hopefully this pressure on companies will lead to fewer such incidents overall. For more information on workplace harassment, please see Chapter 4.

DOMESTIC ABUSE

Domestic abuse, also known as domestic violence, relationship abuse or interpersonal relationship violence (IPV), does not discriminate: it impacts all cultures, genders, sexual orientations, and socioeconomic classes.

TYPES OF ABUSE

Verbal

- Screaming
- Name-calling
- Non-constructive criticism
- Threats to safety and wellbeing
- Being told you are worthless or unintelligent
- Shaming about body type
- Mimicking a partner
- Repeating a partner

Economic

- Needing permission to get money
- Refusing to share financial information
- Refusing to let you do financial management
- Putting all items or property in his or her name
- Being put on an allowance
- Credit and debit cards taken away
- Not allowed to get financial items such as credit cards in his or her name
- Not allowing partner to have a job or earn money
- Taking away or damaging items of value to the partner

Physical

- Pushing, slapping, biting, and punching
- Cornering someone
- Spitting
- Pulling hair
- Blocking an attempt to leave
- Tickling when he or she has been told to stop
- Throwing items at a partner
- Tearing clothes

Sexual

- Rape
- Threatening harm if partner does not engage in sexual acts
- Threatening to cheat if you do not perform sexually
- Ridiculing your sexual ability
- Making a partner "earn" sex
- Forcing a partner into prostitution
- Coercing a partner into sex
- Forcing a partner to participate in a threesome
- Recording a partner's sexual activity without his or her permission

Emotional

- Showing off or cleaning firearms after threats have been made
- Humiliating a partner, particularly in front of others
- Constantly comparing partner to others
- Alienating partner from his or her children
- Accusing the partner of cheating without evidence
- Cancelling
- Ignoring, also called stonewalling
- Saying no one will believe the partner about the abuse
- Putting a tracker on the partner's car
- Threatening to report a partner to social services without just cause

Domestic abuse includes verbal abuse, economic abuse, physical abuse, sexual abuse, and emotional abuse. The goal of the abuser is gaining power and control. As you read earlier in this book, gaslighters thrive on gaining power and control over their victims.

Verbal abuse includes screaming, calling names, being told you are worthless, and getting constant nonconstructive criticism. People that are verbally abusive don't always yell—gaslighters are known for saying very vicious things while they have a smile on their face. Part of the reason for this incongruous behavior is: first, not wanting someone in public catching on to the abuse they are giving out; also, catching their victims off-guard gives them a feeling of control; and finally, if gaslighters are being pleasant, their victims let their guard down long enough for the gaslighters to see an opportunity to strike.

Economic abuse includes gaslighters' requiring that you ask permission to have money, giving you an allowance, not allowing you to have control over the money you've earned, having all items and property in their name only, refusing to share financial information with you, and insisting that they do all the money management, with no input allowed from you. Again, this is all about power and control. If gaslighters refuse to allow you to pay for anything on your own or manage your own money, it's because they know you are less likely to leave if you don't have financial independence.

Physical abuse includes cornering individuals, shoving, pushing, intentionally tripping, pinching, tickling people even after they say to stop, pulling hair, biting, spitting, punching, slapping, or pulling at clothes. Blocking the door when someone attempts to leave can also be considered physical abuse, especially when force is used to stop the person from escaping a dangerous situation. It also includes physical abuse of pets and children.

Sexual abuse includes rape, threatening harm if a partner does not perform sexual acts, coercing a partner into sexual acts, forcing a partner into prostitution, withholding sex, or making a partner "earn" sex.

Emotional abuse includes purposely showing off or cleaning firearms or other weapons when threats have been made, humiliating a partner especially in front of others, saying cruel things about a partner when they are easily overheard, turning the children against the partner, accusing the partner of having an affair without any evidence, canceling plans as a punishment for something the partner supposedly said or did, canceling a partner's plans with friends or family without the partner's consent, telling the partner she is losing her mind, falsely telling the partner that she never said or did something, telling the partner in detail about how great previous partners were, name-calling the partner, and teasing the partner.

Some of the most common tactics used by gaslighters qualify as emotional abuse. Gaslighters know that emotional abuse doesn't leave visible damage, like bruising or scars, as physical abuse can. To gaslighters, emotional abuse is ideal—it is a way of gaining control while still looking like a pillar of the community. A gaslighter may threaten that if the victim comes forward, no one will believe her because he is such a beloved figure. Others in the victim's life may say the same thing: "If you say something, you will destroy his career." It is clear in such cases why victims have not shared their stories.

LEVELS OF VIOLENCE

One of the insidious things about domestic violence is that it doesn't start out with outward aggressive violence. It can begin with partners being possessive, or telling their partner that what she's wearing is too revealing. It can then ramp up to name-calling and shoving. Then it escalates into threatening, then physically harming the partner. If a person does not remove herself from the violent situation, death from domestic violence is a very real possibility. There is no time table to how quickly or slowly domestic violence behaviors ramp up—but what is known is that they do increase over time. The intensity of the violence, how long it lasts, and how frequently it occurs worsen, almost always.

THE ABUSE CYCLE

People who are abusers don't always behave abusively—and that is just one of the reasons that victims find it difficult to leave. If you are with a person who is abusive 50 percent of the time, but good to you the other 50 percent of the time, it can cloud your judgment. Remember that even if a person is occasionally abusive toward you, it is still an abusive relationship. Gaslighters aren't usually 100 percent bad—if only it were that easy. They can still have moments of behaving humanely. (Usually those times are preceded by the realizing by gaslighters that you are on to their game—gaslighters' fear of being exposed kicks in quickly.)

In Chapter 2, you learned how gaslighters start a relationship by "love-bombing" you. They come on way too intensely—the proverbial "sweeping you off your feet." It feels like nothing you have experienced before. They tell you that you are perfect, that you are the most wonderful thing that has happened to them, that they have waited their whole life for you. However, the tide will turn eventually.

When you fall off the pedestal a gaslighter has placed you on, nothing will get you back on it. Nothing. Gaslighters go from idolizing you to devaluing you. Now you can't do anything right, in their eyes. They'll tell you they wonder what they ever saw in you. You may have seen smaller signs of abuse in the beginning of your relationship—a little comment about your weight or appearance, or a comment about how you are clumsy or even not that bright. When you exhibit vulnerability or uncertainty, the gaslighters' manipulating and shaming behavior rapidly escalates.

Now the gaslighters may tell you that your family are terrible, useless people. They may say that your friends are bad influences, and that they dress "trashy" or "slutty." They'll tell you that you always come home with a bad attitude when you visit your friends and family, and you need to spend less time with others for the sake of your relationship. Gaslighters threaten to leave you because you don't devote enough time to them or the relationship. They tell you that this is the worst, most unfulfilling relationship they have ever been in.

If you wonder whether they might be cheating, they'll say that you are crazy and call you paranoid. They tell you that maybe they should go ahead and cheat, because you keep accusing them of it. If you have proof of their infidelity, gaslighters still insist they haven't cheated, and that the person who is messaging them is a crazy ex who is obsessed with him. They tell you that they've wondered about your mental health for quite a while, and that accusing them of cheating proves you have issues.

You say you're going to leave, or that you can't take it anymore. All of the sudden, gaslighters act repentant. They tell you they'll do anything to make things better. They bring you flowers, make you dinner—everything that you have wanted them to do. But they don't really have good intent behind this behavior—they're just worried about losing power and control over you. In Chapter 2 you learned about "hoovering"—gaslighters trying to suck you back in. Once gaslighters know they've got you back under their control, the pattern of abuse returns and escalates again.

This cycle of honeymoon phase to violence to repentance to honeymoon phase never ends. Be aware that every time you go through this cycle, the abuse will become worse and worse. Your best option is to get out of the relationship.

GETTING OUT

Once you stand up to them, you'll see gaslighters change quickly. They will go from shocked, to angry, to repentant. The bottom line is that gaslighters don't want their behavior to become public knowledge. That would ruin their image.

When victims tell a gaslighter they are leaving, or when they say they are reporting the gaslighter's abuse, they are often told:

- "Who would believe you?"
- "I have a powerful job, you are nothing. No one will believe you."
- "You'll ruin your career."
- "You'll ruin my career."
- "Go ahead; everyone thinks you are crazy already."
- "Sure, call the police. You know they're going to arrest you, and not me, right?"
- "They'll arrest both of us. You really want your kid put in foster care?"
- "They'll take the kids away from you."
- "I'll take the kids away from you."
- "Do that, and you'll never see the kids again."
- "You'll have nowhere to live."

- "I'll make sure I tell them about all the times you abused me."
- "What, I don't pay for enough in your life? Who do you think put a roof over your head?"

Some domestic violence victims have recorded the gaslighter's behavior on their phone while the gaslighter berates them. Gaslighters don't want others to see their true colors, so this can stop their behavior quickly. However, it can also lead to the gaslighter destroying the victim's phone, or denying access to a phone. Be careful if you take this route.

A gaslighter who pays your phone bill may say that he has the right to look through your phone at any time. He may also take your phone away so that you have no access to contacting friends and family. If you are planning on leaving, get a second, "burner phone"—a phone whose number you do not give out except to a few emergency contacts. This allows you to still have some form of communication with the outside world if the gaslighter takes your phone away. If you are paying your own phone bill and the gaslighter breaks your phone or takes it, that is considered willful destruction or theft of your own property, and you can file a police report.

Dr. Judith Wuest and Marilyn Merritt-Gray (2016) wrote there are four stages to leaving an abusive relationship: counteracting abuse, breaking free, not going back, and moving on. First, you need to make a plan. Where will you go? Do you have an "emergency" bag packed with essential items, such as medication? What domestic violence shelters are available? What options do you have for legal services? For more information on domestic violence shelters and low-cost to pro bono legal services, see the Resources section at the end of this book.

"I've been threatened, my kids have been threatened—even my pets. I'm working on getting out, but I'd be lying if I didn't say I was terrified."

—Fatima, 38

Leaving may be one of the most difficult things you will do in your life. Your job is to take care of yourself and your children the best way you can—and to never go back to this relationship. You also need to be aware of signs in the future that a potential partner may be a gaslighter and have abusive tendencies. To learn more about red flags of gaslighters, see Chapter 3.

It is imperative that you and your children receive counseling. Most likely you have been through years of abuse trauma, and you need someone to talk to for you to process all the feelings and damage that may have occurred, and to build up your self-esteem and independence so that you do not go back again. For more information on counseling, see Chapter 12.

Be very aware that abusive relationships do not improve. They continue to escalate, many times ending in death. Gaslighters are not people who are going to see the error of their ways, make a heartfelt apology, and work hard to improve themselves. They can talk all they want, but you know they have made no real attempt to get help or improve their violent behavior. Gaslighters are all talk, and will always be all talk. It is time to give up the idea that the two of you can work this relationship out. It ended with the first signs of control and abuse.

SIGNS OF IMPENDING FATAL VIOLENCE

You need to know that getting out of an abusive relationship may be your only chance for survival. If you are in an abusive relationship with a gaslighter, and he has any of the following characteristics, you are more prone to being killed as a result of domestic violence.

- Firearms in the home
- Prior history of domestic violence
- Prior history of any violent behavior
- Family history of domestic violence
- The violent incidents have become increasingly physical in nature
- Verbal threats, not just blatantly stating he will kill you, but also indirect statements, such as "You won't be a problem much longer."
- Affiliation with known violent criminals
- Has abused, maimed, or killed pets, either previously or in your relationship

You need to get out now. You will either leave this relationship, or there is a very real possibility that you and your children will be killed. Peter Jaffe PhD and his colleagues reported in a 2017 journal article that your child is more likely to be killed by an abuser as revenge, upon separation, and if there is a prior history of domestic violence. They also found that more than half of the almost 40,000 children killed each year are killed by their fathers or stepfathers.

So, if you don't leave for your own well-being, at least leave for your child's well-being.

DOMESTIC VIOLENCE AND ITS IMPACT ON CHILDREN

When you are the victim of domestic violence, you have less of you emotionally available to your children. A study by Dr. Mariana Boeckel and her colleagues in 2015 found that the more severe the domestic violence is, the weaker the quality of the emotional bond between mother and child. The weaker the quality of the emotional bond between mother and child, the more severe is a child's post-traumatic stress disorder (PTSD).

If you are exposing your child to domestic violence, there is a greater risk that your child is also witnessing the gaslighter mistreating his pets. A study by Dr. Shelby McDonald and colleagues in 2017 found that domestic violence in the home greatly increases the chance that your child has emotional trauma from seeing a pet be abused. The gaslighter's abuse of a pet was done in a deliberate effort to control the child.

TRAUMA BONDING AND STOCKHOLM SYNDROME

One of the most difficult aspects of domestic violence to understand is that every time an abusive event happens in a relationship, there is a chemical reaction in the brain that bonds the couple together—even when one is perpetrator and one is victim. This is called trauma bonding. What is called Stockholm syndrome can also occur in abusive relationships. This is when an abuse victim feels empathy toward an abuser and will even defend him and his abusive behavior. Trauma bonding and Stockholm syndrome are two reasons that people who are victims in abusive relationships with gaslighters find it so difficult to leave. It can be incredibly difficult to leave; if you recognize yourself in this situation, please see Chapter 12 and the Resources section for additional suggestions on how to get help.

YOU CAN BE ACCUSED BY A GASLIGHTER

The flip side of people feeling safer these days of talking about harassment is that some gaslighters, claiming to be victims of such abuse, make false accusations to punish employers or former partners. Unfortunately, the fact that these are often he said/she said (or he said/he said or she said/she said) situations makes it easy for a false accuser to lie about events that never happened—and it takes legitimacy away from legitimate complaints.

There is no easy way to determine a legitimate from an illegitimate complaint, without hard evidence, such as video. This is one of the reasons that victims of such harassment have not felt comfortable sharing their stories. If you are the victim of a false harassment complaint, consult an attorney.

DATING VIOLENCE

According to the National Sexual Violence Resource Center (2015), one in five women is raped in her lifetime, with eight in ten women knowing their attacker. Date rape is a very real danger, especially when a woman is with a gaslighter. Rape is about power and control, and that is exactly what gaslighters seek. It is recommended that women never leave a drink unattended when out with a gaslighter on a date, to prevent a drug from being slipped in. It is also important that you have an emergency contact—someone that knows that if you send even a blank text, to come to help you. Always let friends or family know where you will be going when you leave for a date. You can learn more about gaslighter red flags in dating in Chapter 3.

If you find yourself in an abusive situation, please know that you are not alone. There are many suggestions throughout this book for dealing with—and leaving—a gaslighter. One organization you can turn to is the National Domestic Violence Hotline (1-800-799-7233 or www .thehotline.org).

———

AS YOU'VE LEARNED, gaslighters come from all walks of life; in this chapter, we explored how a gaslighter who engages in harassment and abuse can be a spouse who has power over you or can be someone who is wealthy, powerful, and who knows he can get away with it. The next chapter looks more closely at some of these higher-profile gaslighters.

6

MAD FOR POWER

Gaslighters in Politics, Society, and Social Media

A S WE'VE BEEN SEEING, GASLIGHTERS WILL CONFUSE, DISTRACT, AND harm so as to get away with behaviors that otherwise would draw attention and outrage. Unfortunately, this is as true for public figures as for private citizens. Think about the damage that can be done when gaslighters take to the big stage of politics, traditional media, or social media. The potential to destabilize, skew reality, abuse, and control behavior and choices soars.

On the national stage, they have the capacity to make or break the rules that hundreds of millions of people live by every day. They can make laws that affect our access to such services as health care, and the safety of our air and water and food supply. That kind of power in the hands of a gaslighting personality is a true recipe for disaster. That's why it's so important that citizens use their sacred voting right and be willing to step up and take action when people in public office are disregarding the needs of the public. But I'm getting ahead of myself.

In this chapter, we will look at how gaslighting operates on the public stage and what we can do to (1) be on the alert for it, and (2) protect ourselves. We'll discuss specifically:

- How politicians gaslight their constituents
- How media organizations also gaslight us by shaping stories for maximum appeal rather than pursuit of important truth
- How social media gaslights by obtaining or spreading information without taking responsibility for it

GASLIGHTERS IN POLITICS

Politicians go into politics for all kinds of reasons. Some enter it with motivation to serve. They want to help fix problems and represent the needs and perspectives of their constituents, to make their community/city/state/country better places for all. They want to help the greatest number and do the greatest good, albeit with varying perspectives on what that good might be. Others have less pure motives. They crave the limelight; they get their kicks from having power and control.

Let's take a look at some of the common characteristics of gaslighting politicians and leaders. You'll notice that these are many of the same characteristics we find in all gaslighters, but their expression is on a different order of magnitude and obviously carries the potential for harm on a greater scale. I'll talk quite a bit about dictators (authoritarian leaders), as they are always gaslighters, but you'll find that there are plenty of examples in our own country and others of nondictator leaders who use gaslighting behaviors, too. With power and control at their fingertips, the opportunities are ripe.

COMMON CHARACTERISTICS OF GASLIGHTERS IN THE PUBLIC SPHERE
They Behave As If They Are All-Powerful

Gaslighters in public office will appear as if they are in total control and expect everyone to do what they say. Dictators and people with strong authoritarian governing styles are perfect examples of gaslighters in power. They can be brought down, of course, but they act as if they are omnipotent.

They Show Little Empathy

One of the hallmarks of gaslighters is their lack of empathy, and in politics it is no different. We see this in the United States, where politicians may help write or vote for bills that will throw people off health care or deprive them of vital services, such as free meal delivery to the homebound or quality education, or stick citizens with exorbitant taxes to line their own pockets. They show an arrogant disregard for other people's needs. This happens abroad as well. One striking example from recent history happened in Venezuela in November 2017. While the people of Venezuela were starving during an economic crisis, with inflation at 3,000 percent, their dictator, Nicolás Maduro, gave a speech in which he pulled an empanada out of his desk drawer, bit into it, and kept talking (Lisi 2017). The media were forced to air the speech (Hayer 2017).

They're Megalomaniacs

Gaslighting politicians do not see themselves as employees of the people. They can even delude themselves into thinking they are saviors for their country. Gaslighters do not think of the greater good when they change laws. They act solely to benefit themselves and the people who support them. And it's no accident that their policies and laws so often end up putting money in their pockets.

They Retaliate

If you dare to cross them, or even make your needs known, gaslighters in power will come after you with a vengeance. They will target you, or even worse, target your family. Gaslighters know that to really get even with you, going after your family makes you suffer the most.

"We do not argue with those who disagree with us, we destroy them."

—*Benito Mussolini*

"I was responsible for everything so I accept responsibility and blame, but show me, comrade, one document proving that I was personally responsible for the deaths."

—*Pol Pot*

They Fail to Take Responsibility

All gaslighters live for power, and they never want to accept responsibility when they abuse it. It is always someone else. They'll blame opponents, they blame the citizens, they blame staff—anyone and everyone else is open for scorn. This isn't a case of not knowing when they've made an error—they clearly do—but they'll always, always point the finger at someone else.

They Detest Intellectuals

Gaslighters in power usually show nothing but contempt for educated people. It's not hard to see why. The educated are the people most likely to speak out against a gaslighter's behavior. Citizens in the fields of science, technology, engineering, and history are particularly detested by gaslighters in power. Why? Because these people have facts to back up their criticisms of the gaslighters. And gaslighters do not like being challenged—especially by facts.

"To read too many books is harmful."

—*Mao Zedong*

They're Obsessed with Optics

Gaslighters know very well that a large part of public perception depends on *optics*—the way an event or person is perceived by the public. Gaslighting politicians will literally and figuratively push people out of the frame or, conversely, inflate crowd numbers to increase their own importance, such as by claiming that attendance at a rally or political event was much larger than it actually was.

They Are Allegiant to Money, Not Citizens

Gaslighters in politics have one primary allegiance—to money, particularly their own. They live and die by the almighty dollar. Don't expect them to vote based on what their constituency wants and needs. They are strongly influenced by the people and organizations who give them money—they vote and govern based on who writes the biggest check. While one may argue that many politicians do this, gaslighters take it to an extreme. It can get to the point where politicians take straight-up bribes, don't even know what their constituents want, nor do they take any time to meet with those they represent. These politicians know who owns them and act accordingly.

US gun laws are a perfect reflection of this pay-to-play, money-trumps-all mentality. According to a 2017 report by the Center for Responsive Politics, in 2016 the National Rifle Association (NRA) gave over $1 million to politicians. Since 1998, the NRA has given $4.23 million to current members of the US Congress (Williams 2017). Take a look at how Congress votes on gun laws by checking out a report by National Public Radio (Kurtzleben 2018)—think that's a coincidence?

Their Words Don't Match Their Actions

While many politicians promise things during election season and don't fulfill them when they get into office, gaslighters take this to an extreme. As you learned in Chapter 1, gaslighters talk a good game, but rarely do they follow it up with actions. One way to check whether politicians, particularly legislators at both the state and federal level, are doing what they say, is to look up how they voted on particular bills. For more information on where to find this information, see the Resources section at the end of this book.

"Politics is when you say you are going to do one thing while intending to do another. Then you do neither what you said or what you intended."

—*Saddam Hussein*

They Turn Citizens Against Marginalized Groups

Gaslighting politicians compare their opponents to the worst evils. These types of politicians feed off people's fear. If you turn people against a particular group—be it a political party, race, age, or culture—by inciting fear, you get those people to align with you. You then also conveniently have a target for all the woes you claim are happening in your country. This ties in to gaslighters' lack of responsibility: blame a group for everything, and turn large numbers of people against them. This ropes in frightened individuals to do the work for the gaslighter. As you read earlier, gaslighters get a high off being able to manipulate people on that scale.

They Seem to Act Irrationally

"Act" is the key word here. Acting outraged can just be a cover, a distractor from the cold, calculating gaslighter personality. The term *crazy like a fox* typifies the gaslighter. Gaslighters know exactly what they are doing. And they know how to work a crowd. If you appeal to people's base emotion of fear, they can be very easily manipulated. Germany under Adolf Hitler is a good example of this. Hitler would whip crowds into a frenzy with his yelling, xenophobic rhetoric, wild hand movements, and exaggerated gestures. He was acting—creating a persona to mesmerize his listeners. And it drew people in.

They Don't Know the Word *Cooperation*

Gaslighting politicians do not believe in cooperation—they pit people against one other to further their own agenda. Except in one key aspect—they do require that everyone under them do what they want—in other words, do as they are told. If staff do not obey, they are met with quick rebuke and can expect to be dismissed at any time. And heaven help the subordinates whose gaslighting boss feels they have gone against him in public. Such bad optics are not tolerated.

They Make People Dependent on Them

If you keep your staff and citizens dependent on you, then you can pretty much get away with anything. They will not question you, even when your behavior is outrageous. If they questioned you, it would mean risking being cut off by you. One of the ways that gaslighting leaders achieve dependence is by initially aligning with a weak ally. Gaslighting leaders get the benefit of riding the coattails of an ally—and by the time they inevitably reach a higher level of power than the ally, the ally is dependent on them. The ally is then sometimes crushed by the gaslighters, now being seen as unwanted competition and expendable. At the same time, gaslighters crave having others depend on them, for it fills their narcissistic needs. For example, Czarina Alexandra Feodorovna, wife of Czar Nicholas II, believed that Grigory Rasputin helped heal her son from the effects of hemophilia. The more dependent Alexandra became on Rasputin (especially when the czar left town to oversee Russian armies during World War I), the more influence he gained over her—contributing to the polarization between the family and Russia's citizens and government (Radcliffe 2017).

Their "Information" of Choice is Questionable

Merriam-Webster (2018) defines *propaganda* as "ideas, facts, or allegations spread deliberately to further one's cause or to damage an opposing cause." Gaslighters are notorious for using propaganda to sway opinion. Of course, they don't call it propaganda. Propaganda can

"What good fortunes for governments that the people do not think."

—*Adolf Hitler*

be anything from not telling the whole truth, using false equivalencies to prove a point, or making broad generalizations that are not based in fact. And this is nothing new. Ancient Greeks and Romans used propaganda to sway public opinion (Jowett and O'Donnell 2018). Usually the "information" is presented in such a way as to scare people, anger them, and/or turn them against a particular group. Again, gaslighters are not interested in facts; their goal is to consolidate and maintain power.

They Try to Rewrite History

Gaslighting leaders hate any symbolism or history that came before them. It's as if they think they can reprogram citizens into thinking that the world started with their reign. It is a form of cultural genocide. This can take the form of destroying religious artifacts or buildings. In 2001, the Taliban destroyed by dynamite a pair of enormous sixth-century statues, the Buddhas of Bamiyan. Seventy years earlier, to enforce the USSR's policy of state atheism, Joseph Stalin ordered the destruction of the original Cathedral of Christ the Saviour in Moscow. Any sign of the past or different ways of thinking are a threat to gaslighting leaders.

They Give Themselves Titles

Not content with just being "president" or "king," gaslighting leaders will give themselves special titles. They use this title as a message to everyone that they are more important than the people they serve. In North Korea, Kim Il-sung (1912–1994) called himself "Great Leader"; his son, Kim Jong-il (1941–2011), was "Dear Leader"; and the present ruler, Kim Jong-un, "Supreme Leader." Gaslighters also tend to use these titles (or their names) in third person, including referring to themselves with the "royal" *we*.

They Project

Projection is a classic behavior of gaslighters, who put their own issues onto others; for instance, a politician may call someone a crook when he, himself, is the one who lacks ethics or is actually breaking the law. Gaslighters accuse an opponent of spreading misinformation about them when they themselves started the smear campaign, just to be able to scoff at or challenge it. It's a classic move to distract—and to hold one's own anxiety about one's faults or weaknesses at bay. It's worth paying attention to what people say about others. It's often quite indicative of how they feel about themselves.

"It is a lie that I made the people starve. A lie, a lie in my face. This shows how little patriotism there is, how many treasonable offenses were committed."

—*Nicolae Ceaușescu*

They Have Reaction Formation

Reaction formation is the psychological term for when people with anxiety and fears about something act as if they are adamantly against it. While reaction formation is damaging enough in families, politicians have the capacity to punish population groups for a behavior they actually share. For instance, a politician who is adamantly antigay rights is then discovered to be gay, one campaigning on "family values" turns out to have had multiple affairs, or a pro-life politician persuades his mistress to get an abortion. In the hands of a politician, reaction formation can not only be an extreme form of hypocrisy but have brutal consequences.

They Repeat Outrageous Lies

Gaslighters are notorious for lying. When these lies are spouted from a politician's bullhorn, it has the effect of eroding the collective sense of reality. They'll repeat their lies over and over until people start to believe them. It doesn't make a difference that there is no credible source to back them up. Also, the bigger the lie, the more you won't notice all the other smaller lies that are sneaking right past you. They do this to destabilize, to weaken our grasp on what's real, and to consolidate their power.

> "There is no state with a democracy except Libya on the whole planet."
>
> —*Muammar Gaddafi*

They Need to Stay in the People's Consciousness

Gaslighting dictators can't stand when they are being ignored. They crave attention. They want to be in people's mind, all the time. They don't care whether it's good or bad attention—they need it like they need air. Attention from constituents or followers gives gaslighters legitimacy. Social

> "I am the object of criticism around the world. But I think that since I am being discussed, then I am on the right track."
>
> —*Kim Jong-il*

media is ripe for giving such politicians what they need: they will make a statement that is outrageous, just to get attention, and it will then be repeated again and again online.

Gaslighting leaders will commission works of art with themselves as the main subject, even when citizens are starving. Remember that gaslighters don't care whether attention is positive or negative attention. To them, attention of any kind is attention. Kim Jong-il commissioned a terrifying number of images of himself, placed around North Korea. Joseph Stalin had statues of himself erected all over Russia.

They Are Obsessed with Symbols

Gaslighters are obsessed with symbols that reinforce their power. They tend to take commonly used symbols, particularly those used by legitimate religions, modify them, and then adopt them as symbols of hate. Adolf Hitler took the ancient religious symbol of a swastika—used in Hinduism, Buddhism, and Jainism—reversed the arms, and made it into the ubiquitous symbol of the Third Reich. Nazis also took to using a character of the pre-Roman runic alphabet, the othala rune; this symbol is now used by white supremacist groups. And although a Celtic cross, a cross combined with a circle, which dates back to ancient Europe, is still used legitimately in Christian religions, white supremacist groups now use an adaptation of it as another of their symbols. The power of choosing commonly used symbols and then giving them a variation is that it is at first subtle, and not seen as "odd" by the general public—however, it acts as a "code" to identify other followers. As this bastardized form of the symbol becomes well connected with a leader or group, it is used to invoke fear and show power of force.

They Use Distraction

Gaslighters know how to play citizens like a fiddle. If an unpopular law is created, they will say something outrageous or pivot the topic so as to distract. A gaslighter will pit people against each other so they are so busy arguing that they don't notice or can't deal with what the gaslighter is doing in the meantime.

They See People as Expendable

Gaslighting dictators see their citizens as means to an end. If someone has to die, then so be it.

> "In any country, there must be people who have to die. They are the sacrifices any nation has to make to achieve law and order."
>
> —Idi Amin

Gaslighters will go to extremes and kill whoever stands in their way. They usually have someone else do the killing, as they feel doing it themselves is "not their job," and they are above such a task. But they have no problems with giving out the orders to kill. They don't like their opponents? They kill them. During Joseph Stalin's "Great Terror," 1.2 million "anti-Soviets" were killed (Ellman 2002).

They don't like what a journalist wrote about them? They kill them. Someone speaks out against them? They kill them. Take, for example, Alexander Litvinenko, a former Soviet agent who openly criticized the Kremlin, including in a book he wrote; became a British citizen; and worked on behalf of British intelligence. Litvinenko was exposed to polonium-210, a radioactive substance, possibly through a cup of tea poisoned by another former Soviet agent. At the time, Litvinenko was looking into the assassination of journalist Anna Politkovskaya, a vocal critic of Russia's war in Chechnya. A public inquiry by the British government found that Litvinenko's poisoning was "probably" approved by Russian president Vladimir Putin (BBC 2016).

> "People who try to commit suicide—don't attempt to save them! . . . . China is such a populous nation, it is not as if we cannot do without a few people."
>
> —Mao Zedong

People are less likely to speak out when they know their life is on the line.

They Appoint Their Family to Positions of Power

Gaslighters' obsession with loyalty is one reason why they put family members in positions of power. They know the family members will be loyal to them—to a fault. Additionally, politicians' secrets are less likely to come out when they have their family in political positions. The family has an emotional investment in keeping illegal and unpleasant activity quiet. Political nepotism is almost always a recipe for disaster for the governed. When a family in power is focused on its own interests, it can run a country right into the ground. Fidel Castro's brother, Raúl Castro, Cuba's defense minister for almost fifty years, was named president of Cuba after Fidel Castro's death in 2008 (Radtke, 2017). Other family members can even be stealing from the government coffers and no one will confront the leader because he has surrounded himself with yes men. Especially when the leader encouraged the heist in the first place.

If you are a gaslighter, you want to surround yourself with people that are afraid to question you or bring up their own needs. Your family is the best bet—your manipulative behaviors have bred a high-level fear into the people closest to you. The more they fear you, the more you can get away with gaslighting the citizens you represent. No one is going to question you.

That said, if a gaslighting leader is caught doing something illegal, or he fears relatives pose a challenge, he will have no qualms about throwing family members under the bus. For example, Kim Jong-un arrested and then executed his uncle, Jang Song-thaek, a senior government leader, and subsequently executed Jang's family and Kim's own half brother as well. A statement released that Jang had engaged in "treachery in betrayal of such profound trust and warmest paternal love shown by the party and the leader." (Ryall 2017; Fisher 2013).

What Can You Do?

What can you do about politicians that trade in lies and can be bought and sold? First, always exercise your right to vote. It is one of the most powerful means citizens have to let their voice be heard.

Educate yourself on the sources of your politicians' funds. There are several websites that keep up-to-date information on contributions. See the Resources section at the end of this book for some of the best ones I know of.

Gaslighters want you to be quiet, to not make a scene. Don't fall for this. Call out gaslighting behavior. When you see a politician displaying gaslighting tactics, such as distracting with outrageous behavior, blatant lying, abuse of power—state the obvious. Social media is a way to let your opinion be heard.

Join organizations with like-minded beliefs. There is power in numbers. Your professional organizations usually have policy committees. These committees commonly organize a day where you visit your state and federal legislators to discuss with them (or their aides) your concerns.

Let your elected officials know where you stand on bills and other issues. There are simple ways to contact them—including via phone or e-mail, or by text bots that fax your representative with exactly what you want to say. For more information, see the Resources section at the end of this book.

Remember that you are paying the salary of your state and federal representatives. You are their employer. If you don't like what you are paying for, vote accordingly.

Let me say it again: It is very important to exercise your right to vote. So many people never get the opportunity. Your vote counts.

How Gaslighting Leaders Ultimately Fail

As we discussed in Chapter 1, many gaslighters eventually fall victim to their own manipulative behaviors. There is always a large chance that gaslighting leaders will do so—because the very same tactics that seek to control other people often ultimately work against the gaslighters themselves. After analyzing 218 events since 1800 where democracy was established after an authoritarian (dictator) regime, Daniel Treisman PhD (2017) found that two-thirds of these events were due to mistakes by authoritarian leaders. He detailed four mistakes that these leaders make which lead to their downfall. The four errors are:

- Calling for elections and starting military conflicts, then losing them
- Ignoring citizen unrest and being overthrown
- Starting reforms that then get out of control
- Picking a secretly pro-democracy person as a leader

You can see how gaslighters are prone to making these errors. They only consider their own opinion, and don't consider the input of citizens and even their own advisers. Gaslighters always think they know best.

One can hope that eventually all dictators will fail due to their fragile egos. Tragically, many times too many people are hurt and killed before that happens.

GASLIGHTING MEDIA

One way politicians control the narrative, of course, is through clever use of the media. And when control of the media—newspapers, radio stations, television—is consolidated into the hands of a few, you've got a perfect vehicle for gaslighting. Not to mention censorship of unpopular opinions. This is why it is so important that media outlets not be allowed to become a monopoly. If only one or two groups own the media, there is a great danger that it will become state-run. Some dictators have taken over a media company by force, whereas others have formed their own media companies. There is also the influence of government on media—while the government may not officially own a media entity, they strongly influence it. In Russia, laws have been enacted that make it easier for the government to censor journalists and block access to websites; in addition, journalists have been threatened and attacked (Slavtcheva-Petkova 2017).

When the government starts telling the media what to write or show to the public, journalists self-censor for survival, or the government blocks Internet access, we're all in serious trouble. Venezuela's president Nicolás Maduro forces the media to broadcast his speeches (Hayes 2017). Many dictators and authoritarian rulers have done the same. And pity the media owner who tries to defy a despot. His operations will be shut down and he'll be imprisoned.

The idea of unbiased reporting, of leaving your viewpoint out except in an opinion piece, which existed when I received my telecommunications degree in the early 1990s, has now become more permeable. And with the advent of social media and more news outlets competing for viewer time, the line between news and entertainment has become more blurred. When a "reality" television star became president of the United States, things really tipped into surrealism.

When the president of the United States orders the media to leave the room while meeting with a world leader, refuses to take questions from particular news outlets, endorses one news outlet and calls the others "fake news" while making over two thousand false or misleading statements all within the first year of his presidency, you know the problem is serious (Kessler 2018; *Washington Post* 2018).

Always Check for Cred

Not only is it vital that we protect our media outlets from being gobbled up or censored, we must all use our good sense and rely only on reputable news outlets. A reputable news outlet holds to principles of *journalistic integrity*. Its reporting relies on a credible source or sources, and if a journalist is offering a personal opinion, it is clearly stated as such. My undergraduate degree is in telecommunications production. Believe me when I say that true journalists and other media are held to high standards of accountability because of their great power to influence others.

Reputable news outlets must also report when they have made an error. For example, recently, National Public Radio (NPR) revealed that its senior vice president for news, Michael Oreskes, had resigned after sexual harassment allegations. NPR reported that there were questions as to when management had become aware of Oreskes's alleged behavior and his alleged past history of harassment at the *New York Times*, and as to whether NPR had acted with due diligence (Kennedy 2017). Here the news organization itself was reporting on its own shortcomings. By contrast, a Fox News website search for Roger Ailes mentions nothing about Ailes's alleged history of sexual harassment or the suit against him filed by Gretchen Carlson, a former Fox News anchor.

That's how gaslighting works in the media: black out the stories you don't like and maybe they'll disappear or be forgotten altogether.

Be a Responsible Poster

Before you post or retweet a news story on social media, check to see whether it is true. Here are some tips:

- Check the source of the story, including its URL.
- Crosscheck the story with reputable news organizations. If it's verifiable, they will have a story on it.
- Look at the source's "About" section on its website. Is it factual or is sensationalist language used? If there is no "About" section, this is a red flag on its legitimacy.
- *Always* and *never* tend not to appear in legitimate news stories.
- If a story quotes a source, look up that source. Is the person or organization cited a legitimate authority, with training in that field?
- If a source quotes a study, look up the study; www.scholar.google.com is a good place to verify published scientific studies.
- If a story has no attributed author, it is suspect.
- Is the story fact or speculation?
- A story that has a question for the title is usually answered with "no."

GASLIGHTING IN SOCIAL MEDIA

Social media has become a ubiquitous part of our lives. It's so alluring to be able to make contact with people in seconds—but it is also a rabbit hole that we can all too easily fall into and get lost in.

Again, the key is to be a responsible consumer. What you read on social media may not just be false—it may also have sinister and manipulative purposes. Think about the extraordinary revelations of Russian hacking and other efforts to influence the US presidential election in 2016. As you may have read, social media companies don't vet (verify) their advertisers, and there are thousands of bot accounts at social media sites. These bots have the aim of manipulating public opinion, affecting election outcomes, and destabilizing society. As Abraham Lincoln said, "A house divided against itself cannot stand." In 2016, the Russian government knew this, and it used social media to create polarization among US citizens.

Social Media Advertising

It is estimated that 126 million Facebook users in the US saw posts, stories, and other content, including advertising created by Russian government agents over the course of the 2016 presidential election (Byers 2017). Facebook initially reported that the content had only reached 10 million US users. It gave information to Congress on three thousand ads linked to Russia. So, not only were the posters engaging in gaslighting activity, but the social media corporations played their part as well. Even if they were unwitting accomplices, I believe they should share the burden of responsibility.

Facebook pages and Twitter accounts with the names "Defend the 2nd," "Secured Borders," "LGBT United," and "Blacktivist" were found to be fake accounts with Russian ties. One Russian-based Facebook page posted cute dog photos—with the possible intent of leaking political content over time (Isaac and Shane 2017).

One example of such ad manipulation was when a Russian Facebook account with 250,000 followers promoted an anti-Muslim protest at a Houston mosque in May 2016, while another Russian account with 320,000 followers encouraged Muslims to attend a counterprotest at the same location and time (Cloud 2017).

Social Media Bots

Between September 1 and November 5, 2016, there were 1.4 million election-related tweets sent by Russian bot accounts (Wakabayashi and Shayne 2017). Bot accounts are fully automated and controlled by code. While some bot accounts are relatively harmless, Russian bot accounts were specifically designed to create arguments among users, with an intent to lead to degradation of US society.

Twitter estimates 2,700 accounts had ties to the Russian-sponsored Internet Research Agency (Romm and Wagner 2017). Reporters and editors from over twenty thousand news outlets around the world retweeted or replied to these fake Russian-sponsored tweets from January 1, 2016 to September 30, 2017 (Popken 2017).

Google found $4,700 worth of ads with questionable ties to Russia. Eighteen YouTube channels were affiliated with the Russian government's disinformation campaign (Romm and Wagner 2017).

Facebook has acknowledged that "most" of its personal accounts have had their personal data scraped by "malicious actors" (Madrigal April 2018).

How do you know when a bot has communicated with you?

- The handle is followed by a list of numbers, i.e., @joe345654434.
- A reverse image search finds that the profile photo was lifted off another account.
- There are no posts on the account.
- The account sends out tweets at all hours.
- The account just retweets content with certain keywords.
- The account consists of just replies to content with certain keywords.
- The account has primarily "click-bait" content.
- The profile photo or banner is overly patriotic.
- The account doesn't ramp up tweets right before an election as legitimate accounts do (bots start tweeting misinformation much earlier).
- Their posts are full of inflammatory statements or rhetoric.

If you see accounts that appear to be bots, report them to the owner of the media. (They will investigate, especially when many people flag the same accounts.) Also keep in mind that many people in power have fake followers on social media—sometimes numbering into the hundreds of thousands or more—so don't take follower numbers at face value.

Protecting Yourself from Social Media Manipulation

Social media companies claim that they have only limited power in who has access to their sites, and that it is almost impossible to track and ban all the offending accounts. These companies want users to shoulder the burden of verifying accuracy and validity. It's too complicated and costs too much to do it themselves. Or so they say.

Report accounts and advertising that looks like propaganda. If you are thinking about joining a group on Facebook, do your research and see who organized the group, and if there are actual people behind it.

With the consumption of information having moved largely online, we are at greater risk than ever of being gaslighted. We are also living in a time where we are inundated with information—and we don't review if the source of the information is accurate and unbiased. It's important that you do some double-checking before you retweet or post any article that has a bias to it. Your best protection from bots is to keep an alert and skeptical attitude, rely only on news sources that follow journalistic standards of excellence, and do your homework.

Resist participating in online surveys or signing petitions, unless you have confirmed that the organization behind it has a legitimate purpose you support; often these exist only to cull as much personal information as possible from participants, and as we know from the Facebook scandal, this can have far-reaching consequences.

A GASLIGHTER OF A DIFFERENT KIND

There's one social milieu that seems as if it were designed by, for, and about gaslighters—cults and other extremist groups, such as ISIS, white supremacists, and Holocaust deniers. All of these group leaders are gaslighters, and cults (the religious type sometimes referred to as "new religious movements" in the press) and extremist groups satisfy every conceivable checkbox for gaslighting behavior. Cults and extremist groups are almost always run by charismatic, media-savvy, and controlling leaders who manipulate their followers into blind obsession. Cults and extremist groups also tend to go against societal norms. They prey on people who are in desperate straits or particularly vulnerable to needing direction and structure and then lead them down the dangerous path to giving over their mind (and what few possessions they might have) to the leader or organization.

—

LET'S TURN TO the next chapter to explore cults and extremist groups, and what you can do to spot, avoid, fight, or get away from them.

7

BEWARE THE MAN BEHIND THE CURTAIN

False Messiahs, Extremist Groups, Closed Communities, Cults, and Gaslighting

W HILE YOU MAY THINK THAT CULTS ARE RARE AND THAT THIS CHAP- ter isn't relevant to you, I encourage you to read it. Any person or organization can exhibit cultlike behavior and can strive to take advantage of you and gaslight you; you may find information here that speaks to your life and experiences even if you think cults are the stuff of news and made-for-TV movies. Additionally, we are hearing more and more about the rise of extremist groups, whose values are based in religion or a particular belief system (such as white nationalism).

Look carefully at closed communities, extremist groups, and cults and you see all the usual gaslighting traits: seductive charm and the promise of taking charge, slowly ratcheted mind control until one's sense of personal agency is destroyed, isolation from loved ones, flying monkeys, and punishment of those who try to extricate themselves, among others. Cults and extremist groups exist in every country, and in every cultural group. No one is immune.

Cults have torn apart families, caused permanent psychological damage, and have gotten members and outsiders killed. They break down a person's psyche and replace it with the prescribed beliefs of the leadership. Cults have long-lasting effects on people's emotional and even physical health—even years after leaving the cult.

That's why I am devoting a chapter of the book to how to spot a cult or extremist group, resist its pull, and get away if you've found yourself mixed up with one (or help a loved one break free). Just like in cases of domestic violence, as you read about in Chapter 5, victims of cults or extremist groups can be trapped in a cycle of abuse and dependence from which it is very difficult to break free.

Some cults and extremist groups are not so much about a belief system or religion—they are about gaining control of people and fleecing them of their money and dignity. Sounds a lot like other forms of gaslighting, doesn't it? In a cult or extremist group, one leader or set of leaders must be followed or else—and the consequences can range from monetary fines to physical punishments or even death. Other extremist groups, such as white nationalists, focus on a particular ideology—and use the hallmarks of gaslighting (lying, distorting, etc., and many of the techniques discussed in the previous chapter) to recruit members.

TYPES OF CULTS AND EXTREMIST GROUPS

There are different types of cults and extremist groups, including political, religious, and destructive. Political cults are oriented around political action and ideology; for example, "far-left" or "far-right" beliefs. Some sectarian political organizations would fall into this category. Religious cults, as the name implies, are organizations that claim to have a spiritual or religious purpose. Some breakaway churches would qualify as cults, as would such groups as Heaven's Gate or the Branch Davidians, both of which you may have read about elsewhere. Destructive cults are less well known. They acquired this label because their goal is to deliberately injure or kill members of other cults. Criminal gangs and terrorist groups would be examples of such cults. (Here I am using the label "terrorist" for any group that uses force or violence against a person or persons to intimidate as part of furthering its agenda.)

This chapter will focus mostly on religious and destructive cults, which are particularly dangerous due to the wide amount of psychological and physical damage they have, can, and will do to members, their families, and society.

Cults vs. Healthy Belief Systems

People will often ask me how you can tell the difference between a cult and a healthy but offbeat or nonnormative belief system. Let us count the ways.

Cults, extremist groups, and closed communities may include the following unhealthy behaviors:

> "I belong to a normal church now, I can come and go as I please. That was really wild to find out, that I could just not show up one week, and that was cool with them."
>
> —*Sadie, 40*

- You are "locked in."
- You no longer have free will.
- You are not supposed to ask questions or to question leaders' authority.
- You are told that the group is superior to other groups and people.
- They'll tell you they can raise your children better than you can.
- They'll sabotage and undermine family relationships, particularly between parent and child.
- Your children are taken from you to be raised by the group's members, and you are told it is in your children's best interest.
- Your children must attend a specific school.
- Older members are married to the cult's children.
- Your spouse is chosen for you, from within the group.
- Money usually flows to the leaders to buy lavish items, while followers live in relative poverty.
- There is no clear accounting of funds.
- You are pressured to give them large or regular sums of money.

- You are told you need to leave your money to the group upon your death.
- You are told to give up all your possessions, and may be encouraged to give them all to the group.
- They operate businesses with other names, and hide their true affiliation.
- They may have splintered off from a legitimate religion due to their extreme beliefs.
- Science is seen as wrong.
- They have a series of strict rules or "laws."
- There is a strict dress code or mandatory uniform.
- Specific ways of eating, sleeping, and interacting are deemed to be for or against the group's norms.
- Specific jargon is used that does not exist outside the group and its members.
- Isolating behaviors are used to keep you in the cult and not divulge information to "outsiders."
- Demeaning names are given to people who are not members of the group.
- Punishments can range from psychological to physical.
- Leaders sexually abuse minors and other followers.
- You are expected to commit crimes with or on behalf of the group.
- Mental health treatment is shunned.
- If you leave the designated buildings or compound for any reason, you are followed or chaperoned.
- A good opportunity for you (a new job, for example) is seen as a threat.
- Your family is told to shun you (cease all communication) if you leave.
- You are stalked and harassed if you leave.

As you can see, many of these behaviors are what gaslighters do. There is coercion and manipulation of others; manipulating for personal gain; emotional, physical, and sexual abuse; and fostering dependency, among others. You may find similarities between these behaviors and those of gaslighters who abuse their partners, as you read about in Chapter 5.

Contrast the preceding list with healthy communities, organizations, or belief systems, where:

- You are not only allowed to ask questions, you are encouraged.
- You are free to leave at any time.
- Your children stay with you.
- The parent-child bond is respected and encouraged.
- There is an administrative body that provides "checks and balances."
- There are reasonable tenets to the religion.
- You are not asked to break laws.
- Healthy family relationships are encouraged.
- You are given guidelines, but not punishments.
- Mental health treatment is encouraged for depression and anxiety.
- There is a clear accounting of funds.
- While there may be a sponsored school, you are not forced to have your child attend, nor are you punished.

Keep in mind that any belief system can become a cult if the dogma becomes inflexible over time, there are punishments for "disobedience," there's an "us vs. them" worldview, and there are consequences for questioning leadership.

CHARACTERISTICS OF CULTS

They Use the First Amendment as a Defense

In the United States, things are not so different. If "outsiders" try to criticize a specific group, they will often be called "un-American" for trying to curtail people's "freedom" or be accused of being "against the First Amendment" by trying to suppress "the free practice of religion." You'll recall that the First Amendment grants people the right to the free practice of a religion, to free speech, and to assemble peacefully. Dangerous closed groups will hide behind the First Amendment, because as a society,

Americans tend not to want to challenge people's constitutional rights. The First Amendment does not apply to groups who are psychologically abusing others and holding them against their will, but that doesn't keep cults or extremist groups from trying.

They Offer Exclusivity

Closed groups also gaslight followers by telling them that there is esoteric knowledge that only the cult possesses. They trade in promoting *scarcity*. Group leaders will add to the mystique by promising that as you rise up through the levels of the cult, you will become more enlightened. It should be noted that one doesn't rise up through those levels easily. It takes an unrealistic amount of time and energy—and in many cases, a large amount of money—to reach the "enlightened" stage.

Scarcity causes people to think only of their own desires and not of the greater good of a community. In a cult, the leader may tell followers that only so many people get to a particular stage of enlightenment—such as that the afterlife has only so many spots for "true believers." The more time you devote to reaching this state of enlightenment, the better your chances of beating other people to it. Interesting how that works. More time, energy, devotion, and money to the group, the more "special" you become. Does that sound like a good deal to you?

> "We were taught that we were the only ones that knew the way to true happiness. But no one really knew how to get there. I was told that I hadn't done enough 'tithing' to get to that place."
>
> —*Marisol, 52*

If a leader truly had the answer to the meaning of life and knew how to become enlightened, you'd think he'd want to share this information with everyone. Healthy organizations operate from an idea of *abundance*; they want others to be happy, whatever path they choose. In closed groups, a scarcity mentality is used as a way to punish and control.

In legitimate religions, not only is there a notion of abundance but a system of checks and balances to make sure one person doesn't become all-powerful. Of course the lines aren't always so clear. Your best bet here, as in all situations where you think you might be dealing with gaslighters, is to go with your gut—if something doesn't feel right, it probably isn't.

They Reinforce "Us Versus Them"

As we've been seeing in each chapter, gaslighters thrive on isolating their victims from others. They convince their victims that they are the only ones who care, and no one "out there" has the victim's best interests in mind. With closed groups, members will start dropping their contact with the outside world, and very quickly they are relying on people within the group exclusively for emotional and financial support. These groups further this isolation along by portraying outsiders as "sinners," "ungodly," or dangerous. This fosters fear, and ensures that people stay within the literal or metaphorical walls of the group.

> "I was raised that everyone outside my church was evil, and we were the only good ones. Everything was a war between us and the outside world. If we questioned our preacher, we were punished."
>
> —*Zamora, 28*

They Use Jargon and "Special Words"

Cults will often reinforce exclusivity by using made up words and language, or they come up with different definitions for words from what they commonly mean. It's another way they reinforce an "us vs. them" mentality. One red flag that you are dealing with a cult is if you ask a cult member what a word means, and the person can't tell you, or refuses to explain it. This insider jargon is part of a strategy to make members feel that they are much more "enlightened" and intelligent than the rest of us.

> "When I got out, I had to learn how to talk like a regular person. I didn't realize how many words I used that were just part of my church."
>
> —*Loretta, 43*

They Expect Public Professions of Loyalty

Gaslighters use social consistency to their advantage. Cults, for example, commonly have members profess their loyalty in front of as many

"I tried to run away, and as punishment I was brought in front of all the elders and made to recite the rules, and repeat back what my punishment would be if I tried to leave again. I had to repeat back that the only way to a godly life was through the church."

—Ramona, 48

other members as possible. When you announce to a hundred people that you will be faithful to the group and its leader, you are making a social contract with everyone in that room. Gaslighters know that people don't like to be seen as inconsistent, and will use these public demonstrations as often as possible to cement loyalty.

They Won't Answer Questions Directly

Evading questions is another hallmark of gaslighters. Ask anyone who has ever tried, as a noncult member, to ask a cult leader what goes on within the group, and you'll discover that such questions are never answered. People are told that they just wouldn't "get it," meaning they aren't as smart or enlightened as those in the cult, or that only members may be party to such information, or their questions are answered by questions thrown right back at them. Dare to question the group's beliefs while you are a member and you will be punished for questioning. Ask a leader a question about the legitimacy of the cult, and you may well be told you are violating human and constitutional rights.

They Force You to Marry Within the Cult and to Have Kids

Leaders will encourage (or force) members to marry within the group. This ensures both members' ties to the

"My minister told my now-wife and I that we were getting married. I didn't even really know her very well. People at my church weren't even allowed to date. I never questioned it because I was taught my minister was always right."

—Jason, 40

cult and decreases the chance that they will leave. Furthermore, what better way to reinforce the group ideals than by having your spouse there to remind you of them? Further controlling your personal life, most cults will pressure you to have children to increase their numbers. If you do have kids, the group may take your children away so they can be indoctrinated. A child born into a cult is highly unlikely to leave the cult.

They Engage in Brainwashing and Foster Stockholm Syndrome

Cults will carefully dismantle your belief structure through gaslighting and coercion, and replace your beliefs with theirs. They need you not to think freely for yourself. Sometimes this is referred to as *programming*, and it can take years to "unprogram" yourself from the thought and belief structure of a cult. This phenomenon of hostages developing sympathetic feelings or attachments to their cap-

> "It has taken me a long time to be able to do things that are normal for everyone else but outside of the church's rules, and not feel really uncomfortable about it."
>
> —Jeannette, 45

tors is called Stockholm syndrome. People with Stockholm syndrome often don't want to leave their captors, even if given the chance.

Members of cults are a lot like hostages and can suffer from this as well, due to the ways they are psychologically manipulated into feeling bound to the cult—through fear and punishment. It is much like an abusive relationship, which you can read more about in Chapter 5.

They Won't Allow You to Leave

As with all gaslighting relationships, cults do not always seem very cultish at first. And then, by the time you realize you need to get out, it is usually too late. Cults will use extreme measures to keep members from leaving. Some cults have even been known to threaten to get family members of cult members deported if the member tries to leave. Some will hold passports hostage so followers can't leave. Some cults will physically stop people from leaving.

Cult Leaders Don't Live by Their Own Rules

The rules are strict and the punishments severe, but don't expect leaders to live by the same strictures. While followers may be told that they need to live a life of austerity, for instance, numerous cult leaders have been known to spend followers' money on lavish lifestyles. They may tell followers that sex is not allowed outside of marriage, while they are having sex with multiple followers.

They Replace Your Values with Theirs

To belong to a cult, members often experience "cognitive dissonance." They'll realize that their own values and beliefs are in conflict with what they are being taught. Cults have methods of breaking people down and replacing their values and beliefs with the cult's own.

When we are confronted with beliefs that are different from ours, we have several choices:

1. Ignore the new conflicting information.
2. Commit even further to our existing beliefs.
3. Avoid exposure to contradictory information.
4. Project our feelings of overwhelm onto others.
5. Absorb the contradictory information and change our existing beliefs.
6. Accept the contradictory information as it is and accept holding two different beliefs.

Of course, cults will try to get you to choose number 5. They'll attempt to brainwash you, often through intimidation, telling you that your family and friends are worthless or "sinners," and the cult (and only the cult) can offer you a way to reach a higher state as a human being. You will no longer be able to think for yourself. Individualism is stamped out. The cult becomes all-powerful and always right, with no room for "gray areas."

They Prey on Our Desire to Belong

People with personal difficulties and difficult histories tend to be the most vulnerable to the promise of feeling complete and healed and taken care of, and cult leaders can smell this from a mile away. Cult leaders prey on feelings of outsiderhood and in fact often isolate people so they will be less and less likely to reenter, or even be interested in reentering, mainstream society. If you are lost and need a metaphorical compass to follow, cults provide that. At a very steep price.

In many cases, cults present themselves as helpers to lure potential members, who will then be "groomed" into a relationship with a cult member, ideally the cult leader. Once a new recruit forms a relationship with a cult member, especially the leader, it is much more likely they will stick around. And get indoctrinated.

They Scam Members Out of Money

Cults will also take your money and then not use it as they said they would. If you attempt to ask for proof of where it went, you will be accused of being a blasphemer or threatened with excommunication. Giving over your money is often a requirement of membership. In fact, some cults will tell you that you can't advance to the next stage of development or enlightenment until you pay a certain amount of money as a sign of your loyalty.

They Engage in Forced Labor and Human Trafficking

Many cults also engage in human trafficking. Human trafficking has been referred to as modern-day slavery, and there are an estimated 20.9 million victims in the world, with 90 percent in forced labor and 22 percent in forced sexual exploitation, and 5.5 million are children (International Labour Organization 2012). Labor trafficking consists of bonded labor, forced labor, and child labor.

> "They took my passport. There was no way for me to get out. I was forced to work and beaten every day."
> —Ruby, 23

In bonded labor, a victim is forced to work off a debt. For example, cult members are given fliers and books to give out in their recruiting efforts. If they're discovered not to have given out all their materials in a given day, the members are forced to do extra work to pay off their "debt."

Forced labor is when a victim is forced to work under the threat of violence or other punishment.

Cults are also notorious for child labor, in which children are forced to work, including in unsafe conditions and at all hours of the day and night.

"I was told I had committed sins against God, and was forced to work in a labor camp to 'redeem' myself."

—*Niamh, 38*

One might even say that cults are de facto human traffickers in that they don't let members out of their sight, they punish members for not "obeying," and cult leaders will claim that members owe debts to the cult (Boyle 2015). People are forced to stay in the cult through fear and punishment.

They Will Use Many Means to Destroy the Opposition

Cults are famously litigious, going after people that speak out against them, sometimes filing lawsuit after lawsuit against them—with the purpose of bankrupting them. Many times, the cults have succeeded in financially wiping out the people they see as opposition. They will also attack opponents through smear campaigns intended to incite fear and suffering, and decrease the chances of the person or entity speaking out against them again. It's also a warning sign to anyone else who tries to defy the cult or call them out on their practices.

Another trademark of most cults is their ability to hunt down those who try to leave. The cult will make various attempts to come after you, if not physically, then through attacks on your credibility. This is what gaslighters do.

WHAT TO DO IF A LOVED ONE IS IN A CULT OR EXTREMIST GROUP?

If you have a family member in a cult or extremist group, please know that it is usually very, very difficult for followers to break free. They have been brainwashed into believing that the leader and the cult or group are the only ones who love them and care about their well-being, and they may resist all efforts of help. But that doesn't mean you shouldn't keep trying. You can ask law enforcement to do a "wellness check" on your loved one. Also consider contacting an attorney if you feel your loved one is no longer capable of handling her finances or other responsibilities.

Some mental health professionals will caution you to start small when contacting a family member in a cult. Do not initially challenge the cult's beliefs and don't expect long outings or meetings. Keep them short and manageable. As you start rebuilding rapport with her, visits and contact may grow, albeit slowly. Remember that progress is still progress, even if it is by just inches. Be careful not to make statements about how wrong the cult is or how it is hurting your family. This can cause your loved one to immediately withdraw or go into defense mode. Reconnecting your family will be a slow process. Mental health professionals can help you with how to approach her and possibly heal your relationship. Patience is key. You can learn more about counseling in Chapter 12.

It is important to educate yourself about gaslighting, cults, and extremist groups. Learn how these organizations operate, and how they lure in members. Also learn details about the cult or group your loved one has joined. The more you know, the more likely you will be able to educate her (and counteract cult brainwashing) during an intervention with her.

What starts the process of a person leaving a cult or extremist group? There are six main triggers, according to a 2017 study led by Kira Harris, PhD: social conflicts within the cult, a change in cult dynamics, having conflicting emotions about roles in the cult, the leadership of the cult not following cult rules or expectations, pressure from police, and family influence. So, family does play a role in a member leaving the cult. Also, presenting your loved one with such information as print or media articles or videos showing that a cult leader's behavior is incongruent with cult rules can help initiate the process of leaving the cult.

If a family member is contemplating leaving a cult or extremist group, it is important for her to know that upon exit she has a safe place to stay, social support from family and friends, and possible opportunities for earning income. The more you can show that you have these safety and security concerns taken care of, the more likely it is that your loved one will eventually exit the cult.

However, let's say you've been patient and tried all these things. It can be easy to become completely consumed by working at getting your family member out of the cult. Establish boundaries where you will say "enough is enough." You can love someone, but also detach and acknowledge that she has made life decisions that have impacted your emotional, physical, and even financial health—and it's time for that to stop having such an influence on you. You can't "make" someone leave a cult or extremist group.

For more information on organizations and mental health professionals that help former members of cults and their families, see the Resources section at the end of this book. A legitimate organization or mental health professional is one that is cited in scholarly work, such as journal articles, and the head of the organization and its board are licensed, certified mental health professionals.

WHAT TO DO IF YOU ARE IN A CULT

If you are in a cult or extremist group and have found a way to get access to this book, that is amazing. You must have gone through a lot to get ahold of it. Please know that there is hope for you, and a life with meaning and happiness outside the cult. Know that the cult cannot legally keep you against your will. Their doing so would be what is known as false imprisonment.

The first thing to do is create an exit strategy, but tell no one in the cult about it. The cult may already sense that you are straying, so be aware of attempts to control you further or isolate you away from other followers.

Try to reach outside communication. Be aware that if you are contacting outsiders from within one of the cult's buildings, your calls may well be monitored. If you do succeed in leaving the cult, check to be sure you aren't followed. And if you can, report any suspicious behavior to law enforcement.

Once you do leave, please get counseling. If you've been in the cult for a long time, you will face adjusting to life on the outside, as well as a likely history of abuse and neglect, deprivation of education, and difficulty emotionally attaching to others (Matthews and Salazar 2014). You can do this. Take it slow. You can learn more about counseling in Chapter 12.

—

LET'S MOVE ON from cults and extremist groups to gaslighting family members. They can make you question your sanity and do quite a bit of harm to you. It's hard to get away from them, as well.

8

THE ONES WHO REALLY
GET UNDER YOUR SKIN

Gaslighters in Your Family

A S YOU'VE LEARNED IN OTHER CHAPTERS, GASLIGHTERS SHARE A LOT of similar behaviors. However, there is something about gaslighters in our families that make them some of the most exasperating ones to deal with. They have some particular characteristics and tricks in their toolbox, as you'll see. Also, our histories and emotional ties with these people mean we often can't just get away from them so easily, especially when we're young. And even later on, they're often present during holidays, family reunions, and they may live near you. They can be like a constant festering sore. And they usually know exactly what buttons to push to get you going—and they thrive off the ensuing chaos. You may have noticed these issues with gaslighters in your family.

> "My stepdad gaslights my mom all the time. He says stuff to her, and then will say, 'No, I never said that.' I'll tell my mom I heard exactly what he said the first time, but now she's telling me I just don't like him and I'm trying to drive them apart. I can't stand it."
>
> —Liam, 20

In this chapter, we'll look at how to spot the gaslighters in your family and what you can do to protect yourself.

Confronting Doesn't Work

Gaslighters will never own up to their bad behavior. When you confront gaslighters in your family, they may say something like "You're being too sensitive" or "You've never been able to take a joke." And don't be surprised if they tell other members of the family, in front of you, what just transpired. They want to embarrass you as much as possible to "get even." Stand your ground. It takes a lot of courage to be the one to call out gaslighting behavior. Find support elsewhere, if you can, but by all means persevere.

> "My aunt always talks about how crazy and wrong everyone in the family is. Has my aunt ever considered that she is the crazy one? Hell, no. And I'm not going to be the one to tell her. That lady is scary."
>
> —François, 28

They Ruin Holidays

Gaslighters will often take holidays as a special opportunity to wield their chaos like a can of mace. Gaslighters hate when people are happy. Happy people don't need them, and that drives them crazy. Gaslighters will use their full bag of tricks to bring chaos to what should be happy events. They'll triangulate and split during holiday gatherings. They will pit people against each other. They will tell a very embarrassing or inappropriate story about you in front of your family (or the new partner you brought home to meet the family), even after you ask them to stop.

> "My dad took Thanksgiving dinner as an opportunity to tell all our relatives what a 'pain in the ass' I was and told them that I cried for no reason. I could see their looks of pity. I didn't even bother to say something back. There was no point. I was nine years old."
>
> —James, 25

Gaslighters are also notorious for buying inappropriate and cheap gifts. They will spend money on themselves, and even flaunt what they bought for themselves, but they will give you something so flimsy that you couldn't even give it away. Most of the time the gift also has nothing to do with your interests or who you are. Gaslighters have difficulty seeing people outside of themselves. And part of their MO here is to send a message punishing you for being an independent, happy person.

They Force You to Do Things for Them

Family gaslighters want to make you feel that you have free choice, when you really don't. It's the classic "damned if you do, damned if you don't" scenario. If you don't comply with a request, you are tormented. If you do comply, you always somehow get it wrong. Granted, you

> "I pretty much just shut myself in my room growing up, because if my mom asked me to do something, it was always done wrong, or I didn't move fast enough. I wasn't even looking for a 'thank you', just no criticism for once. If I wasn't up and moving within 10 minutes of her asking me . . . . it was really bad."
>
> —Gerard, 44

truly do have a choice—gaslighters can't really make you do anything. But after you've lived with gaslighters most of your life, it can feel very much like that choice has been taken away from you.

They Are Likely Addicts

If you think about what you've read so far, you can see that gaslighting is itself a kind of addiction—addiction to the thrill of gaining power by controlling and destabilizing. If you have addicts in your family, they are more likely to be gaslight-

> "I couldn't tell you when my dad is drunk. I've never seen him not drunk."
>
> —Heath, 25

ers than are others. Addicts have just one concern: getting their next fix. That's just the way addiction works. The need for the substance hijacks higher-order thinking. So, what does this mean for you?

The addict-gaslighter will gaslight you to the hilt to try to guilt you into giving them money or even your possessions. Don't fall for it. You can bet you will never see your money or possessions again. If someone in your family is an addict-gaslighter, do not let that person into your home alone. Change your locks. Keep your valuables in a safe-deposit

> "I walked on eggshells around my dad, especially if it was 5 pm or later. I knew that's when 'happy hour' started. I tried to become invisible."
>
> —Saul, 34

box, in your name only. Do not keep any medications in your medicine cabinet in the bathroom. Keep them in a secured, locked, fireproof box that has been bolted to the wall. Addicts will tell you they will go to open houses just to clean out the medicine cabinet. Consider getting a security system for your home.

They Use Flying Monkeys

Not everyone in the family is going to see gaslighters the same way you do. Don't expect other family members or friends to understand. Back in Chapter 2, we talked about "flying monkeys." These are the people gaslighters will use to bring you back into the fold. Friends and family members are perfect for this role. Gaslighters tell them what to say to you and you do it. Flying monkeys will also often act as snitches, reporting back to the gaslighters anything you say about them and other facts and details about your life. If you tell a flying monkey that a gaslighter was abusive toward you, for example, she will take that back to the gaslighter, who will likely tell the flying monkey a story about how you are the truly crazy one.

It's generally not a good idea to tell other family members or friends why you are distancing yourself from a gaslighter. Family bonds are often too strong, and you are likely to end up getting criticized or ridiculed for limiting or cutting off contact with the gaslighter. But here's what you need to remember: *You do not need to defend yourself.* Your decision is your decision is your decision. You have a right to limit or cut off contact with anyone for any reason.

Gaslighters Have Placaters

There is usually one person in a family who will try to smooth things over with a gaslighter. They get upset when others confront the gaslighter or otherwise make him upset. They have become conflict avoidant as a survival strategy. If you are a placater, ask yourself why. Are you afraid of the gaslighter? Are you not sure what is normal behavior and what isn't? If you have been living with a gaslighter for any length of time, you may not even be sure what constitutes normal behavior anymore.

When you placate a gaslighter, it can cause an internal conflict for you. You may feel an inner rage due to the fact that you aren't "allowed" to express how you really feel. To do so would mean incurring the wrath of the gaslighter.

> "I read something about sociopaths, and I was like, that's my sister to a T. When I call her out on something shitty she's done, my mom immediately runs over and tells me how I need to be nice to my sister because she's had such a hard life. Hard life? Are you kidding me? She's never worked a day in her life, and my parents pay for everything."
>
> —*Naima, 22*

Gaslighters Can't Be Happy for You

Gaslighters try to undermine achievements that signify your independence of them. If you are the first person in your family to go to college, for instance, gaslighters might tell you that you are wasting your time, or that you think you're better than everyone, whereas healthy relatives would encourage you to further your education.

They may also send mixed messages, as Lonnie's mother and Jacob's mother did in our examples. They will ask for something from you, and when you deliver (no pun intended), gaslighters will either dismiss it, tell you they never asked this of you in the first place, or act as though you're burdening them. It is very confusing when you are asked for something repeatedly, work hard to fulfill the request, and then discover you still haven't met expectations.

> "My mother kept asking us when we were going to give her grandchildren. Finally, after years of trying, I was pregnant. When we told her, the first thing she said was, 'Don't expect me to babysit.'"
>
> —*Lonnie, 30*

But here's the bottom-line truth: When you are dealing with gaslighters, you will never be able to make them happy or fulfill their needs. It is impossible. That's part of the pathology.

"My mom told me I had to go to law school. She said anything less than that was 'settling.' She never went to college. I graduated near the top of my class. My mom said at graduation, 'I don't know why you're so excited, it's not like you're going to get a job.'"

—Jacob, 33

They'll never be happy for you and nothing you can do is ever enough.

These methods of gaslighting are more or less unique to families or other close relationships, where people have an emotional purchase on you. Your manager or coworker is not quite in the same position to get under your skin. Your congressperson or president doesn't have the constant presence in your life or the emotional strings to pull, though they can make you plenty hopping mad and off-kilter.

When Bad Things Happen, Gaslighters Don't Become Good People

One would think that when something bad happens to a gaslighter or someone in her family, you would see some glimmer of redemptiveness or kindness. Nope. The gaslighter will gloss right over it and continue on whatever jag she's on. Bad things do not make gaslighters nicer, nor does it make them change. This can be very confusing for family members, who think, "Hey, maybe this [name your bad news] will finally get them to reevaluate life or how they treat

"My mother was complaining about something, as usual. I had enough and told her I had a miscarriage and was not in the mood. She was angry with me for not telling her earlier, then she went right back to complaining again."

—Holly, 28

people." That day of reckoning and reevaluation is never coming for gaslighters. Which, for you, means letting go of the expectation that things will change.

GASLIGHTING PARENTS

Our parents can also be our gaslighters. Healthy parents are supportive and nurturing. They provide guidance for their children so they become happy and productive adults. Some of healthy parents' happiest moments are when their child succeeds at becoming a healthy adult.

However, gaslighting parents manipulate, undermine, and compete with their children—meanwhile, trying to prevent them from being independent people. In this section, you'll learn how gaslighting parents impact your ability to function as a happy, healthy adult.

> "When I was about 15, my friend said that my parents fought a lot. I said, "Your parents don't do that?" She said no, that they got into arguments sometimes but they didn't scream at each other and call each other names. It was the first time I realized not everyone's parents acted like that."
>
> —Lluvy, 35

If one of your parents was a gaslighter, you may find that you just don't seem as happy or fulfilled as your peers. You may also find that you tend to get into relationships with gaslighters more often than others do. We learn how to interact with the world through watching our parents. If your parents got through life manipulating and meddling, chances are you saw that as normal behavior.

> "I grew up thinking there was something wrong with me because I remembered stuff that my mother swore never happened. I thought maybe I was crazy."
>
> —Rafael, 65

They Don't Like It When Children Individuate

Individuating, becoming independent from your parents, is a normal, healthy part of human development. It means that you are learning how to go about the world on your own. We first experience individuation as toddlers. "The Terrible Twos" are characterized by saying no a lot. The preteen and teen years are also times of individuating. Nongaslighting parents see these times as frustrating, but they know deep down that you becoming your own person is a good thing.

To gaslighters, individuation means that their grip on you is loosening—and they hate that. You may have noticed that a parent was pretty nice to you until you hit the preteen years, usually around when you start puberty, and then suddenly started making snide comments to you or ignoring you or stonewalling. What happened? The gaslighter realized you were no longer his "mini-me," and

> "I clearly remember the first time I really said no to my mom when I was a teenager. Why do I remember it so well? Because she stopped talking to me for a month."
>
> —Paulina, 45

> "My dad is a master at stonewalling. I have no idea how he can just treat us like we're not even there. It's so cold."
>
> —Charlotte, 28

instead of bearing up and seeing puberty as a normal developmental stage, he viewed it as the beginnings of abandonment. And gaslighters cannot bear that.

They Are Notorious Abusers

Abuse takes different forms: physical, emotional, sexual, and neglect. If you are the child of a gaslighting parent, you may identify with more than one of these forms of abuse. With the gaslighter, these behaviors may have just seemed like a normal part of life. If you were abused, it is important that you talk to a mental health professional about it. Remember, *the abuse was not your fault*. Full responsibility lies on your gaslighting abuser.

They Put You in a Double Bind

A double bind is a "damned if you do, damned if you don't" situation. You are given two conflicting messages from your parent. For exam-

> "When I was a teenager, my mom would tell me that I was 'getting pudgy.' Then she'd make brownies or cake, and leave it out on the kitchen counter."
>
> —Jalisa, 34

ple, she harps about you needing to lose weight, then makes a big batch of brownies. Or she tells you that you need to get ready for school immediately, but then hands you your portable gaming device. Double binds cause emotional distress, and set people up for failure. For gaslighters, watching you experience tension reinforces to them that they can control you.

They Compete with You

Gaslighting parents, especially of the same gender, will compete with you, often in really unseemly ways. You get a new outfit with your work money when you are a teenager, so your mom has to get a similar outfit. This copying behavior continues into your adulthood. It goes beyond getting something similar so they can share in your experience. For the gaslighter, it is about not wanting you to have better things than they do. You get a new car, so your gaslighting parent has to get one, too. They can't stand being what they see as "outdone."

Healthy parents are happy that their children are achieving—it is in part, a reflection of good parenting and their children's *own* hard work. Gaslighters have trouble accepting that success not necessarily genetic, but something their children have earned.

> "I started dating an attorney, and my mother started dating an attorney a month later. I got a specific type of car—my mother got the same car right afterward. They say imitation is the sincerest form of flattery, but in this case, it was just creepy."
>
> —Sascha, 30

They Try to Live Through You

Not only will gaslighting parents try to compete with you, they will also try to live through you. You may have been pushed to date before you were ready. You may have wanted to join chess club, but a gaslighting parent wanted you to play football instead, since he didn't make the team when he was in high school. While it is normal for parents to want for their children what they didn't have, for gaslighters it's a pathological need to live through their children.

The gaslighter is also the parent who can be found yelling at his child or the referee during his baseball games and other sports. This has nothing to do with supporting you or sticking up for you. It has to do with the gaslighter's needing his child to win, at all costs. If you buy into it, this can mean that you become an adult who is constantly trying to please that parent, even if it involves breaking laws to do it.

A gaslighter's child will never, ever live up to the gaslighter's expectations. They are impossible to reach. By design.

They Have Inappropriate Boundaries with Your Partner or Friends

This one often gets my clients particularly up in arms. When you would bring home your boyfriends or girlfriends, would your parent flirt with them and/or tell embarrassing stories about you? Classic gaslighting behavior. Or maybe your gaslighting parent dressed provocatively when you brought friends over. Did your parent try to buddy up to your friends and be "one of the gang"? Gaslighters can't stand not having as much attention as their children. They see them as competition for others' affection. They would love nothing more than to have your partner or friends fawn all over them. This is part of their narcissistic and insatiable need for attention.

> "My mom would always make some inappropriate comment to my boyfriends, right in front of me. It was mortifying. I started making excuses to my boyfriends about why they couldn't go inside my house."
>
> —Shelley, 43

Golden Children and Scapegoats

In many families where one or both of the parents are gaslighters, one child is the "golden child" and the other is the "scapegoat." The golden child gets away with murder, while the scapegoat child gets punished for the smallest infraction. These patterns can last until through adulthood, causing strife between you and your sibling. A pathological competition between siblings can result. Be aware that each person's role might change or switch without warning: one week you are the "good kid," then, inexplicably, the next week you are the "bad kid." Sometimes it doesn't matter which is which to the gaslighter. This is due to the fact that gaslighters idealize and then devalue people, as you read in Chapter 1. They lack a fundamental understanding of the nature of human beings: that all people can have various aspects to their personality. Gaslighters see a child as either all good or all bad—nothing in between—according to what they want from the child in the moment.

> "My brother always got brand-new toys for Christmas. I always got hand-me-downs. My parents paid for all of my brother's school. They told me I was on my own."
>
> —Maurice, 70

Part of stopping this cycle is identifying it, and realizing that there is no logic to your gaslighting parent's behavior. You and your sibling were unwittingly tossed into a maelstrom of emotional abuse. If your sibling is not a gaslighter (we'll talk more about gaslighting siblings on pages

146–149), it might be time to have a talk and bring out into the open the pathological behavior your parent had toward you. The chances are that your sibling felt just as slighted as you. Just saying that your parent was difficult to live with can help start a conversation.

They Frequently Threaten to Cut You Off

One of gaslighters' tricks for when they feel you distancing yourself from them is to threaten to never speak to you again, throw out your belongings, or disown you (cut you out of the will).

These are most likely false promises. Go ahead and see whether they can do it. Let them threaten not to talk

> "Every other week my mother would threaten to cut me out of her will. Once she even made me give her the house key back, saying she never wanted to see me again. That lasted until she realized I was the only person helping her out. She had alienated everyone else."
>
> —*Donna, 68*

to you. It might be one of the most peaceful times in your life. Eventually the gaslighters will contact you—usually when they need something. It can be difficult to come to terms with the fact that you are an object to be used by the gaslighters to fulfill their own needs. But at the same time, it should be a relief to finally know clearly what you are dealing with.

In regard to disowning you—you may find that the gaslighter really doesn't have much to leave you anyway. Gaslighters are notorious for being poor financial managers. They spend so much money on trying to make themselves look good that they don't save up for the future. If a gaslighting parent dies, even if you are on good terms, you will often discover that you weren't left anything anyway.

> "My whole life my dad threatened to disown me because I was such a 'bad son.' So, I worked my whole life on trying to make him happy. It turns out he didn't leave me anything in the will anyway."
>
> —*Dante, 45*

Have You Gotten Fleas?

You may have noticed as you've been reading this book that you are perpetuating parental behaviors that you told yourself you never would.

But realize that it is normal for children of gaslighters to pick up some of what they witnessed or were subjected to as children. After all, from whom do we primarily learn how to act? That's right, our parents.

The gaslighting behaviors you learned from your parents are called "fleas" because, as the saying goes, "If you lie down with dogs, you will get up with fleas." Please don't beat up on yourself. Just because you picked up some coping techniques and manipulative techniques as a way to survive in your environment doesn't mean you are a gaslighter yourself. But it is true that these behaviors are now maladaptive, as you no longer need them as an adult. As a kid, you may be trapped and vulnerable to having all boundaries crossed; as an adult you have license to set your own boundaries.

Here's the thing. If you think you are a gaslighter, chances are you probably aren't one. It's the people who don't think they are gaslighters who truly have a problem. According to Brooke Donatone, PhD, in her article "The Coraline Effect" (2016), children of people with personality disorders may be misdiagnosed with personality disorders themselves. This is due to the fact that they may exhibit personality disorder behaviors due to not learning adequate coping skills. As you read earlier in the book, gaslighting behaviors are very common in people with Cluster B personality disorders—narcissistic, histrionic, antisocial, and borderline. If you have been diagnosed with a personality disorder and your parent had the same disorder or a similar one, please consider getting reevaluated. If you think you are a gaslighter, see Chapter 11 on how gaslighters can get help for themselves.

Signs that you picked up fleas from a gaslighter:

- You lie about things that you really have no need to lie about.
- Life feels odd or uncomfortable when there is no drama going on.
- You will manufacture drama in your relationship for it to feel normal.
- Instead of stating your needs to others, you expect them to read your mind.
- You find it easier to manipulate people into doing what you need instead of directly asking them.

- You are attracted to people who are emotionally distant.
- You find yourself using some of the same parenting "techniques" as your gaslighting parent: punishing your child for not knowing or meeting your needs, communicating primarily through yelling, stonewalling; or obviously favoring one child.

It is important that you seek counseling if you are the child of a gaslighter. You may find that children of gaslighters have similar behaviors to adult children of alcoholics (ACOAs), and resources for ACOAs may be helpful to you. This is especially the case if you had a gaslighting parent with an addiction, as many do. For more information on counseling, see Chapter 12.

Your Gaslighting Parents and Your Children

If your parents are gaslighters, you need to take precautions with your own children. Please don't leave your children alone with gaslighting grandparents. It's not safe. I've heard of gaslighting grandparents giving chocolate to diabetic grandkids. I've seen gaslighters tell their grandchildren that their parents are mean for not letting them have sweets. They'll take your kid to the park when you asked them not to. They'll buy presents for your child when you said your child had misbehaved and wasn't to go to the store. When you confront your gaslighting parents about these things, they'll say something like "You just don't let her have fun like the other kids." Often, and quite intentionally, within earshot of your child.

> "I come home from work and my kids are watching a scary movie while my father-in-law is watching them. He knows my youngest gets terrified. It's almost like telling him no makes him make sure he does it."
>
> —Nia, 38

If left alone with your children, gaslighting grandparents may:

- Undermine your rules
- Not follow your child's dietary restrictions, such as in the case of food allergies

- Not give your child medication
- Tell your child that you are not a good parent

Gaslighters love attention and drama, and nothing comes close to the attention and drama of going to the emergency room with your child. Gaslighters may feign forgetfulness or confusion when confronted, but this is a cover for the sinister intent of their behavior. Make no mistake, *gaslighters are hurting your child intentionally*. For the attention and power.

> "My mother-in-law knows my daughter was allergic to strawberries. She calls me from the emergency room, saying she gave her strawberry ice cream. She does not have dementia—she just loves the attention. We never leave the kids unsupervised with her now."
>
> —Jackie, 35

Caregiving for Your Gaslighting Parent

You may be in the position of caregiving for an ailing or dying parent. As you may have guessed, illness or even dying doesn't make gaslighting parents any better. In fact, they just seem to get worse. It is really something to see a person at death's door still managing to utter a snide comment.

Gaslighting parents may refuse to take their medication as prescribed, or won't take it at all. They also may not follow their doctor's instructions. They may tell you they know to take care of themselves better than the doctor does. And gaslighters actually believe this. It can be maddening trying to take care of people who appear to have such little regard for their own health.

> "My mother is really sick, yet she insists on taking her medication her 'own way,' and doesn't follow through with the doctor's instructions. Then when I try to help her, she screams at me and tells me I'm worthless."
>
> —Pam, 45

You have a choice in caregiving for a parent. You don't have to be a caregiver. You are *choosing* to be a caregiver. You may be thinking, "But there's no one else to take care of her, I'm it. She's alienated everyone." It is still your choice to be a caregiver. When you realize it's your choice instead of mandatory, caregiving can be a little more tolerable.

It is still not acceptable for a parent to verbally or emotionally abuse you, no matter how sick he is. I don't care whether you are the last person on earth available for your parent—that type of treatment is never okay. If you

> "My mother has some mild disabilities, but she does things to sabotage her health. She then expects me to run over to her house, and gets furious when I can't do that right away."
>
> —Seth, 40

are being abused, it's time to reach out and find someone to at least take over some of the caregiving. If you feel you can't afford it, see the Resources section at the end of this book for more information on taking a break from caregiving.

When Your Parent Dies

Many people feel relieved when a gaslighting parent dies. And that can be confusing or induce some feelings of guilt. But it is really perfectly normal. It is also normal to experience something called "complicated" grief. This is grief that is compounded by feelings of anger and unfinished business with a parent. I recommend that you seek counseling to talk about these complicated feelings. If someone tells you that you aren't grieving the "right way," know that there is no right way to grieve. Grief may be universal, but how we feel it is unique to each person. If your gaslighting parent was very good at hiding her manipulative behavior, people might tell you they don't get how "fine" you are with her death. Keep in mind that they did not live with her, so they don't know the real story.

How do you respond to comments about what a wonderful person your parent was, and that you are not grieving properly? The best reaction is none at all. Don't say anything. Would it help to tell them about how horrible your parent really was? No,

> "I felt such a weight off my shoulders when my dad died. Then I felt incredibly guilty about that. It wasn't until a friend said to me, 'You are free now, and you deserve that,' that I felt less guilty."
>
> —Elisa, 48

they will tell you how that can't possibly be true. You don't need yet another person denying your reality.

In the *Reno Gazette-Journal* (2013), I came across this obituary for a mother who had died:

> She is survived by her 6 of 8 children whom she spent her lifetime torturing in every way possible. While she neglected and abused her small children, she refused to allow anyone else to care or show compassion towards them. When they became adults she stalked and tortured anyone they dared to love. Everyone she met, adult or child was tortured by her cruelty and exposure to violence, criminal activity, vulgarity, and hatred of the gentle or kind human spirit.
>
> On behalf of her children whom she so abrasively exposed to her evil and violent life, we celebrate her passing from this earth and hope she lives in the after-life reliving each gesture of violence, cruelty, and shame that she delivered on her children. Her surviving children will now live the rest of their lives with the peace of knowing their nightmare finally has some form of closure.
>
> Most of us have found peace in helping those who have been exposed to child abuse and hope this message of her final passing can revive our message that abusing children is unforgiveable, shameless, and should not be tolerated in a "humane society." Our greatest wish now is to stimulate a national movement that mandates a purposeful and dedicated war against child abuse in the United States of America.

"It wasn't until my mother died that I truly felt at peace. The first Christmas without her was really wonderful."

—*Anna, 45*

GASLIGHTING SIBLINGS

What can be just as damaging as a gaslighting parent? Your gaslighting siblings. As you've learned in this chapter, you and your siblings can pick up characteristics of gaslighters from your parents' behavior (getting "fleas"). However, sometimes siblings are complete gaslighters unto themselves. They don't just have a few gaslighting behaviors—they are the embodiment of gaslighting. First, we'll talk about gaslighting's effects on siblings, then we'll talk about siblings who are gaslighters.

Fierce Competition

As mentioned earlier, your gaslighting parent may have set up a "scape-goat" and "golden child" scenario with you and your sibling or siblings. You may have been in a years-long battle with a sibling over who is "better." You may be constantly trying to outdo each other. You buy a special gift for your mother for her birthday, and the next week your sibling has bought something more expensive. Gaslighters are never appreciative of gifts anyway, but that's beside the point. You and your sibling are still vying for the approval and attention of your gaslighting parent. Your parent has set things up this way since your childhood, pitting you and your siblings against each other. There are few things gaslighters love more than people battling to impress them.

"My older sister started conning me early. She would ask me to do bad things and told me she would pay me if I did. She never paid me, and I always got in trouble for doing what she asked me to do. She would lie to my parents and say she had nothing to do with it, while I got punished."

—Brianna, 24

Be aware that this competition is a false one—everyone has their own strengths and faults. By constantly competing with your sibling, you probably haven't gotten to know each other as people. You will never fully win your parent's approval—so, why not get to know your sibling on a different level? As you read earlier in the chapter, you and your sibling may have picked up gaslighting behaviors as a survival mechanism while within your parents' household, but aren't true gaslighters. You may discover from really getting to know your sibling that the two of you just were in a no-win situation as children, and you may actually really like each other. It's never too late to make a fresh start.

Your Brother's Keeper

When you were a child, you may have tried (many times in vain) to protect a brother or sister from the wrath of a gaslighting parent. Many children of gaslighters, now adults, feel incredibly guilty that they couldn't do more to help their sibling. However, gaslighting parents can be so powerful with their manipulation that many times there was really nothing more you could have done to prevent your sibling from being targeted. Keep in mind it was not your responsibility as a child to protect the other children in your home. That was your parents' responsibility, and they failed.

If your sibling is a gaslighter, it can be maddening when you look back at the times when you protected him from essentially turning out like a gaslighting parent. You may feel that there is an utter lack of appreciation from your sibling toward your "rescue" efforts when you were children. Here you worked so hard at protecting him, and he is making a concerted effort to make your life more difficult. Unfortunately, this is where you realize that you can't control some things in life—and that includes how your siblings turn out as adults. You may never get the validation that you want from your sibling, and that is okay. You know that you did what you could.

Keep in mind that if you grew up fearing a gaslighting parent and knowing you could never share your true feelings with that parent, as an adult you still may have that fear. Sometimes when you can't express your feelings to the person you are upset with, you let it out on your next closest person—your sibling. This may be the case with you and your sibling—is your sibling a gaslighter, or is he taking out his anger with your parent on you instead? It may be helpful for you and your sibling to attend therapy together to sort out your childhood damage—and work on healing your relationship.

Fake Florence Nightingales

Gaslighting siblings will often take on the "hero" role and supposedly devote themselves to an ailing or injured parent. Keep in mind that this "rescuing" is largely an act—your sibling wants to look like the good guy. He has no problem taking all the credit even if you are the one actually taking care of your parent.

If your gaslighting sibling actually has "stepped up" to become a caretaker for your parent, watch him like a hawk. Gaslighters have been known to take advantage of elderly or ill parents. They attempt to turn the parent against the other siblings in the hopes for more money or possessions when your parent dies. Your sibling may also be taking money from your elderly or ailing parent. If you suspect this is happening, or if your parent is suddenly paying more attention to your sibling and calling him out for praise, I recommend that you hire an attorney and/or financial professional to look over the finances and caretaking arrangements of your parent to protect her from being taken advantage of by the gaslighter.

> "I thought when my mother got sick that she would at least act a little better. Nope. She got worse."
>
> —*Caterina, 31*

If your parent has dementia, it is even more important to have a system of checks and balances set up so your sibling does not turn her against you and your other siblings. If your parent is in a state of confusion, it's like an irresistible invitation for the gaslighting sibling to move in and strike.

Siblings and Parent Death

When your parent dies, watch out for a gaslighting sibling's trying to take over. He will go against what is written in the will and steal items meant for you. And don't be surprised to discover that your parent recently changed her will to favor this sibling. Your options are to confront the gaslighter or take him to court. You know from past history that confronting your gaslighting sibling yourself will not get you anywhere. Legal representation may help you. See the Resources section for pro bono legal resources in your community. This situation is particularly tricky if your gaslighting sibling, the "golden child," was named executor of your parent's will.

GASLIGHTING CHILDREN

Sometimes children start manifesting gaslighting behavior, even when they didn't have a parent who was a gaslighter herself. Being the parent of a gaslighter is a heart-wrenching existence—seeing your own flesh and blood cause repeated suffering to others (including yourself). If this is you, you may already have spent sleepless nights wondering, *What did I do wrong?* Part of the heartbreak of having a gaslighting child is giving up the dream of who you thought your child was going to be. It is also very normal for you to be angry with your child.

Let me suggest a few things you can do to take care of yourself.

Forgive Yourself

First, to make progress, know that this was not your fault. *Sometimes people are just born with bad wiring.* Forgive yourself for any blame you feel for having your child turn out this way. If you picked up this book, I'm willing to bet you did everything in your power to make sure your child was happy and healthy.

If you did contribute to your child's gaslighting by behaving in gaslighting ways, remember that as adults we are completely responsible for our own actions. If your child is now blaming you, he's trying to absolve himself from all responsibility, and that is not acceptable. Whatever you think you did to any of your children, *they are still 100 percent responsible for their behavior.*

If you think that you are at least partly responsible for your child's gaslighting behavior, consider consulting a mental health professional (MHP) or therapist. The burden of guilt is a heavy one, and it can sway your judgment and even impact your physical health. A therapist can help you sort out your feelings—and many times it's healing just having someone really listen to you. Let the therapist know the extent of your child's behavior. Give examples of the behavior you've seen. Also give your truth about what you feel is your responsibility regarding that behavior. A therapist can help you sort out what is your responsibility or what you "own" and what is not.

You can attempt to apologize to your child for any feelings of wrongdoing on your part, but keep in mind that your gaslighting child is probably not going to respond in a way that you would prefer. Talking over an attempt at reconciliation with a mental health professional beforehand is a great way to establish realistic expectations and even do a run-through of what you would say to your child. Role playing with the therapist on how your child might react can be very helpful before taking the step of attempting reconciliation. If you are considering therapy for you and your child together, ask your therapist who he recommends. It is important for you to have your own therapist. Another alternative is asking the therapist about having your child come in for one of your sessions. For more on counseling and therapy, see Chapter 12.

If you are financially supporting your child, whether by giving him money or letting him live in your house, *stop*. You are under no obligation to support your adult child, unless your child is disabled and unable to support himself.

Take a long look at your child's ability to support himself. The chances are he could if he truly wanted to—but you have given him no incentive to do so.

When you kick your child out of your house or your wallet, be ready for all sorts of insults to be hurled your way. Your child may tell you that he is only in this situation because of you; that you are being cruel and unreasonable; that you are crazy; or that he will never speak to you again. Remember that you are kicking him out of the house so the manipulation stops and so that you have some money to live on in the future.

Make Your Will as Specific as Possible

If you have a gaslighting child, and especially if you have other children, appoint a neutral third party, such as an attorney, as the executor of your will. If you have items of value, list specifically which item goes to which child or other family member. *Do not leave the dividing of items up to your children.* I've seen firsthand a situation where a gaslighter stole all of her recently deceased mother's jewelry against the will's stipulation that she and her sister divide it equally.

Consult an attorney about your estate and will. Do not have your children attend this meeting. Disclose to your attorney the issues you have had with your child. It is okay to tell the attorney this—in fact, it helps him create a will that is in your (and your children's) best interest. He will also know ahead of time what is up when your child comes by unannounced about some "important information."

In your living will or on health proxy forms, consider naming a neutral third party. You probably don't want the gaslighter to be the one to decide whether to discontinue your life support.

Do not let your child bully you into naming her the executor of your will. She is not wanting this for your good—she is doing it to take advantage of you, take your money and belongings, and shut out her siblings from receiving anything. Gaslighters are slick, and will use all manner of manipulation to get you to name them executor. They may:

- Tell you about the untrustworthiness of your other children
- Tell you that your belongings and money will be given to the state
- Say that they will cut off contact with you if you refuse
- Tell you that you "owe them" this after your treating them poorly
- Tell you that you will no longer see your grandchildren

Respond that an attorney as an executor will make life much easier for everyone after you pass away. Keep repeating this. Do not waver.

If Your Child Is Still a Minor

If your child is still a minor, it is imperative that he be given counseling. Believe in the benevolent dictatorship school of parenting: Your child may have a say, but you have the final decision. If your child needs counseling, he needs counseling. Period. Does it matter that he doesn't want to go? No. He goes anyway. You also need to go to counseling. Your possible lack of boundaries may have led to the amplification of your child's gaslighting behavior.

Aside from counseling, children who are already displaying gaslighting behavior need structure and limits. All children want guidelines for how to behave—the laissez-faire parenting method of letting kids do what they want has been found to not work. So, first take your child to see a mental health professional; next, you need to see a mental health professional as well. Then be willing to impose structure and limits and make these very clear. It may take strength you didn't know you had, but you do. You can do this. And in the long run, it is nothing but good for everyone involved.

WHAT TO DO ABOUT GASLIGHTING FAMILY MEMBERS

You may have conflicting feelings about gaslighters in your family—you want to get away from them as far as possible, yet you feel a sense of guilt for not wanting to be around them. These are very common feelings.

Decide Whether You Really Want to Attend Family Gatherings

The ideal solution is to stay as far away from gaslighters as possible. Gaslighters rarely change, and you don't need to subject yourself to their manipulations. You have the right to have a peaceful life. Your health and well-being come first.

> I learned not to share any personal information or feelings with my mom. I knew it would be held against me in an argument, or just whenever."
>
> —*Ara, 45*

If going away somewhere during the holidays on your own helps you feel better, then do it. *You have permission to do whatever you need to do to be healthy.* You don't get bonus points for subjecting yourself to emotional torment.

If You Must Go . . . .

If you feel compelled to attend a family gathering where a gaslighter will be present, try viewing the experience from the perspective of a sociological researcher. View your family's interactions as a type of data collection. What patterns do you notice?

If the gaslighter tries to bait you and get you upset, respond with confusion. Saying "I'm really confused" when the gaslighter asks you a pointed question will frustrate her—and she is likely to move on to the next person. Yes, there is a chance that the gaslighter will up the ante and exacerbate (worsen) her behavior—be prepared for this as well.

When you feel yourself starting to respond with anger, take a walk outside or simply get up from the table and find a place to take a break. Remember, the gaslighter doesn't "make" you feel a certain way—you are in full control of your emotions. If you need to excuse yourself, by all means, do it. The gaslighter will try to guilt you into staying. She may even threaten cutting you off if you leave. You do what is in your best interest—and getting out of a pathological situation is what is best for you.

> "My mother threatened that if I left Christmas dinner she would never speak to me again. I figured that wasn't a bad trade-off."
>
> —Jerusha, 19

Picking Your Own Family

One of the hard lessons many of my clients have learned is that just being related to someone doesn't necessarily make them family. One of the perks of being an adult is that you get to choose. You can form your own family from close friends—an "intentional family." There is no set definition of family—it is whatever you make it. If you are observing holidays without your gaslighting family members, create new traditions.

Remember, there is life without your gaslighting relatives. Often your best bet, however hard it may feel in the short run, is to get away and stay away. You have no obligation to stick around for abusive gaslighting behavior, and the sooner you can make good boundaries and move on with your life, the better off you will be. If you can't get away, practice building better boundaries. Get counseling. Consult a lawyer and/or accountant for advice on protecting yourself and your family if a parent falls ill. Form an intentional family. Life

> "I try to remember just because I'm biologically related to these people doesn't mean they're my family. I decide who is family."
>
> —Leo, 28

doesn't need to be a series of confusing and excruciating encounters with crazy-makers. It's time to work on seeing things more clearly and to move on.

———

SOMETIMES WE CHOOSE our own family, through our friendships. However, friends can turn out to be gaslighters—and can drag you down with them. In the next chapter, you will learn how to identify a gaslighting friend, and what to do to get out of an unhealthy friendship.

9

WITH FRENEMIES LIKE THESE

Gaslighting in Friendships

PERHAPS IT GOES WITHOUT SAYING BY THIS POINT IN THE BOOK THAT people we consider our friends can gaslight us, too. The word *frenemy* comes to mind. This colorful word describing friction-filled friendships has become so common that in 2010 it was even added to the *Oxford English Dictionary*, with this definition: "a person with whom one is friendly despite a fundamental dislike or rivalry." Doesn't this sound like your friendship with a gaslighter? He does things that really, really bother you, but you hang in there. You get nothing good from the friendship—likely because you got used to gaslighters early in your life and this seems normal. You might think, *What would I do without this "friend"?* Well, for starters, you would have a happier life!

In this chapter, you'll learn how to handle gaslighting friends and neighbors—people with whom, through choice or chance, you may have more day-to-day contact than you do with your relatives. We'll look at the particular dynamics of these relationships and how to protect yourself from their destruction.

Like all gaslighters, gaslighting friends feed off of human misery. They are emotional vampires—you feel exhausted after spending time with them. They want to know all about the terrible things that have happened to you—in great detail. Then, they pay little attention when you want to tell them about something good. Gaslighters have no interest in what is going well for anyone else. They see your successes as ways that you are "one-upping" them. You are their competition. This is because gaslighters view the world as having limited resources. They erroneously believe that if you are having success, there is less success available to them. They can't grasp the concept that being happy for the people around them can also lead to their own greater happiness and success. Tragic for them, but that doesn't mean you have to put up with it.

Beware the Gossip

Gaslighters are terrible gossips. They love learning unfortunate tidbits of people's lives and sharing it with others. It is the fuel they thrive on. It gives gaslighters a feeling of power and control over others. People's personal information is like currency to them—sharing it gets them attention they crave. The difference between your run-of-the-mill gossiper and a gaslighter is that the gaslighter uses the information about others as a way to gain power and pit people against each other, whereas the gossiper is usually more of a *yenta,* or busybody. The gossiper is just passing information to others (albeit inappropriately), whereas the gaslighter wields information like a weapon.

> "I had a miscarriage, and my gaslighting friend wanted to know about it in detail—how much I suffered, and how much pain I was in. She would come to my house unannounced. Then, when I had my baby, she was nowhere to be found. She didn't even call to congratulate me."
>
> —*Sondra, 30*

If you suspect that a friend is a gaslighter, think about how he talks about other people to you. Does he gossip about them and seem to thrive on their misfortunes? This is a sure sign of a gaslighter, and I can guarantee that he is talking about you to them, too. If you think you're being gaslighted and you don't relish the idea of being the subject of gossip, be sure to limit the amount of information you disclose to this friend. Don't give him any ammunition. In addition, if he does start to gossip about someone else, don't stand there and listen. Your silence is a form of complicity. You're saying that hurting others is acceptable to you.

> "My neighbor would tell me about another neighbor's problems with her husband. Right then I knew to never tell her any stuff about me."
>
> —*Amanda, 25*

It's human nature to gossip. It makes us feel connected and important. But stop and think about what it would feel like if the target was you. What if you were to discover that something personal you'd told a friend in confidence had been spread around? You'd probably feel betrayed and hurt. Gossip doesn't sound so enticing anymore, does it?

A good rule to follow in general, but especially with gaslighters, is to not talk about a person if that individual is not present. There are also ways to stop gaslighters when they are gossiping:

- Say, "I don't know whether she would want me to know that."
- Change the subject.
- Walk away.

One word of caution here: Don't think you can change gaslighters' dishing about other people who are out of earshot. Gaslighters will never stop gossiping—they will just move on to another person so they can "spill the beans."

Don't Take the Bait: Splitting and Lying

You'll remember from Chapter 1 that gaslighters are great at splitting. They will purposely pit people against each other. They love to see a fight, and get excited by the fact that they made the fight happen. One of the most common ways gaslighters practice splitting

> "My so-called friend would tell me what other friends said about me. It was some vicious stuff, and understandably it got me so upset. I'm not even sure they said those things. I'm thinking my 'friend' was lying."
>
> —*Lynn, 37*

is by telling you that a friend said something unflattering or unkind about you. The gaslighter will either try to bait you by saying, "I heard something about you today," hoping you will ask what that "something" was, or they will directly tell you, "Susie said she doesn't like how you treat your kids." Gaslighters are particularly fond of saying someone was criticizing your parenting skills. They know that gets people really riled up.

You may be really tempted to find out what Susie said about you. First, keep in mind that unless you heard something directly from Susie, chances are that the gaslighter made it up. The gaslighter is betting you will go up to Susie and say, "How dare you say I'm not a good parent." Susie will most likely say in return, "I never said anything like that!"

If gaslighters tell you someone said something about you, automatically assume it is false. Gaslighters have no problem lying, especially when it means having greater power over others. This is because if gaslighters don't have anything to gossip about, they will make it up. One of the most dangerous facets of their propensity for gossiping is that they don't care whether they are spreading lies. Gaslighters know that people are curious about what others are doing, so they will immediately make up gossip as a way to distract from their own bad behavior. This is a technique they will use especially when you were about to call them out on their behavior.

When gaslighters hint that someone said something about you, they are "baiting" you. They are betting you'll go for that bait like a hungry fish. If you take the bait, this gives gaslighters a tremendous feeling of power. So, how do you refuse to take the bait? By saying "oh" or "okay." When your gaslighter says something like, "I heard something about you from Sally," just saying "oh," with a flat affect will usually stop the gaslighter in his tracks. If he tries to bait you again, use the "broken record" technique—repeat "oh" or "okay" until he stops. And really, who cares whether someone said something about you? People are free to say whatever they want about anyone. As they say, *What other people think of you is none of your business.*

> "I had a gaslighting friend who would constantly tell me that mutual friends were talking about me. Finally I just told her, 'Oh, that's nice,' whenever she started up. She stopped doing it eventually. I guess she got bored of my nonresponse."
>
> —*Harvey, 42*

Another reason gaslighters practice splitting, besides to pit people against each other, is to isolate you from others. Gaslighters would love nothing more than for you to view them as your only friend. That way, gaslighters think, you will devote all your attention to them. Gaslighting friends will even go so far as to use splitting to try to isolate you from your spouse/partner and family. They will tell you that your spouse said something unflattering about you. Gaslighters know that most people will stew over this and eventually explode. They'd love to be the cause of a fight between you and your spouse. Don't give them that power. If a friend tells you that your spouse said something harsh about you, it's always best to check it out with your spouse—or forget it—rather than to give in to the temptation to think the worst.

Their Real Goal in Befriending Your Spouse or Partner

Gaslighters will often go to lengths to form a special bond with your spouse/partner. Be very wary. Do not tell gaslighters when you are going out of town without your spouse. Gaslighters will find a way to get your spouse alone with them. They will text your partner that they need help at their house and possibly show up unannounced at your house. They will pretend to be a good friend to your spouse, and will emphasize how good they are at listening. Gaslighters know exactly what many people in long-term relationships want to hear. This has nothing to do with whether you have a healthy relationship or not—anyone wants to feel listened to and needed. Even if you have a solid relationship, gaslighters have an uncanny ability to know what your spouse might need to feel better about herself. Gaslighter detect it and hone in on it. It is all part of a game to gaslighters—they are never truly empathic or supportive. They just want to find a way to get closer to your spouse.

> "My husband showed me a text from my gaslighting friend, saying that she needed help with her dishwasher. This was followed with a winking emoji. My husband texted back the names of some appliance repair people. She never contacted him again."
>
> —Hannah, 28

Gaslighters will focus on stealing your spouse, particularly if you have disclosed that you are having problems in your relationship. Whatever information you tell the gaslighters, they will use that to get your spouse hooked. If you confided in gaslighters that you are having medical issues, they may say to your spouse, "It must be really difficult having a spouse that is sick." They may also subtly (or not so subtly) point out their own good health—"I'm so glad I work out every day." Their goal with these comments is for your spouse to be aware that there is someone "better" out there who is less of a "burden." Gaslighters don't need to come right out and say it—inferring it is enough.

As we discussed in Chapter 1, gaslighters will slowly ramp up their behavior; they know it's easier to manipulate people that way. If a gaslighter knocked on your door and said to your partner, "Hi, I'm going to sleep with you," it wouldn't nearly be as effective as a slow ramp-up. Instead, the gaslighter will build emotional intimacy with your spouse over time. They are practicing the "cognitive empathy" we looked at in Chapter 1, working from what they think a person should feel and not how they really feel, because they don't have the capacity for real empathy.

These friends will "groom" your partner. They will slowly increase their visits when you are not home—and how odd that their washing machine breaks only when you are out of town. At first, gaslighters may not make obviously flirtatious or sexual comments—it may just be a smile or a compliment. The next time, there are innuendos, then standing too close, up to full physical contact.

Sure, there may be times when it appears that a gaslighter and your partner are just hanging out as friends. However, gaslighters almost always have ulterior motives. Never trust them alone with your spouse. There's just no good reason why gaslighters would need to spend time with your spouse while you aren't there.

You may want to warn your spouse about the gaslighter. "There's something off about Betty. If she comes to the house while I'm gone, please don't let her in," or "I think Betty is trying to hook up with you—please don't go to her house if she asks you to fix something. We need to set solid boundaries with her." Your spouse may say, "Don't be silly, Betty is just a nice person. She's a single mother and needs the help." Your response? "I've seen behaviors that are concerning to me. I will go ahead and give her a list of people that can do home repairs." Keep in mind, again, that people love attention. Gaslighters can act so sweet and innocent, and it's understandable that your spouse may not see them as destructive.

How can you be sure you're not just having your own issues with jealousy? With a gaslighter, you'll have seen a pattern of deceitful behavior. Maybe you've seen a gaslighting friend manipulate other people. Maybe she has tried pitting you against another friend. It's reasonable to assume she lacks boundaries. Maybe you've heard about her hitting on other people's partners. If, when you see how your friend behaves around your spouse, you get a gut feeling that there is something amiss, trust your instincts. They are almost always right.

The lesser goal here is to separate you from your spouse—so you'll have more time to devote to the gaslighter. The greater goal, however, is to "steal" your partner away from you. The gaslighter sees taking your partner as a game to be won. She doesn't care about you, your spouse, or your relationship. She certainly doesn't care about your feelings. As we've seen, gaslighters are serial cheaters. Do you think they really care that they are destroying a relationship and family? No. In fact, they live off this kind of "winning."

If your spouse does wind up having an affair with a gaslighter but wants to work things out with you, seriously consider ending the relationship. Once your spouse breaks off the affair with the gaslighter, things can get ugly very quickly. Gaslighters will stop at nothing to destroy your family if they feel they've been "wronged." Never mind that they wronged *you* in the first place—that fact is lost on gaslighters.

If your spouse has run off with a gaslighter, the joke is on him. When a gaslighter "steals" a spouse, it's as if she has a new toy. It's fun for a while, and then she tosses that toy in the pile with the others. Meanwhile, you have dodged a bullet. You can actually be thankful that you got to see the true character of your spouse.

Whatever happens, remember that this affair is not your fault. The responsibility fully lies with the gaslighter and your spouse. Gaslighters are amazingly good at faking empathy, and your gaslighting friend will likely know exactly what to say that will attract your spouse. There is probably nothing you could have done to prevent this turn of events. Just try to learn from it and avoid the same dynamics in the future.

When Your Child's Friend Has a Gaslighting Parent

"My daughter had her friend over to play. I knew her mom was manipulative and I had really distanced myself from her. I didn't think it was fair to punish my daughter and her friend for the mother being crazy though. That night I get a phone call from her mother, screaming and cursing at me. She accused me of not watching the kids, and that her daughter had bruises on her. I swear, when that child left my house, there was not a mark on her."

—Rosa, 34

A particularly tricky gaslighting dynamic is when your child's friend has a gaslighting parent. Say this parent has shown that he doesn't have good boundaries. He shares school pickup and drop-off with you. If you confront the gaslighter about his lack of boundaries, instead of answering you directly, he may "forget" to pick up your child for school. He may get you involved in some classroom drama with other parents. He may pit you against other parents, or even school administration. Your name may "accidentally" be taken off a parent volunteer list or other important roster, and later you find out that the gaslighter told your child's teacher that you had requested to be removed. The method is passive-aggression. The goal is to punish you and to cause chaos.

If you drop the gaslighter as a friend, you will be inconvenienced with having to do the school transport all by yourself. But more problematic is that you will still need to see this person at school events and parent organization meetings. Cutting off contact with a gaslighter like this can put you in an inconvenient and uncomfortable situation. However, not cutting off contact means your child still has interactions with the gaslighter—and that can lead to big problems down the line. You can tell the teacher that the gaslighter is to have limited contact with your child, and that the gaslighter is not authorized to send along any messages from you. The gaslighter is certainly not allowed to pick up your child from school, for any reason, no matter what he tells school staff.

You will also have to deal with the potential difficulties of having the gas- lighter's child in your life. For example,

"My daughter's friend told me that she thought about wanting to die. I immediately called her mother, who is a very manipulative woman. She told me her daughter was just being dramatic! I told her this was really serious, and I would call 911. She screamed and screamed at me, I can't even repeat the things she called me."

—Emily, 43

driving the gaslighter's child in your car or having him at your home also opens you up to possible liability. You will get blamed for some- thing that the gaslighter said happened to his child, whether or not it ac- tually did. Gaslighters love blaming and getting revenge. While you may feel bad for the gaslighter's child, and as a decent human being want to support the child in some way, it is not a good idea.

It is not uncommon for gaslighters to accuse other adults of harming their child. If you are accused, you are stuck—you may have no witnesses except the gaslighter's child. That sweet child, who you felt sorry for and invited into your home, will lie about you as if their life depended on it (after all, they learned how to survive at the gaslighter's knee). What are you to do? Take photos of the gaslighter's child when he leaves your house to show he has no marks or bruises on him? It's an impossible and dangerous game to play. This only goes two ways: you can either stop having the gaslighter's child in your home or car or open yourself up to having the gaslighter accuse you of neglecting or abusing her child. The choice is clear.

First, tell the gaslighter that because of these false accusations, it's in both of your best interests to no longer have the gaslighter's child in your home. When you frame this action as being best for both of you, the gaslighter will usually put up less resistance or make less of a scene. How do you explain to your child that his friend can no longer come over? One option is to hold off talking about it until the issue arises. Let's say your younger child says she wants Johnny to come over after school tomorrow. You could say, "I'm sorry, that's not possible. Let's come up with something else we could do." Younger children are easily distracted, and are ready to move on to the next thing. If your child is older, you could say, "I don't think that's a good idea."

If your child pushes, you can respond with, "Some things have happened that make that not a possibility." You are under no obligation to tell your child the details—nor does she need to know all that information. Keep in mind that whatever you tell your child may get back to the gaslighter's child, and then to the gaslighter. The more you make it a big deal, the more your kid will make it a big deal.

WHY DO GASLIGHTING FRIENDS BEHAVE THIS WAY?

Gaslighters see friends as commodities or things. They don't see a need for having a reciprocal or "even" relationship with people. They see friends as stepping-stones and a way to get what they want.

Lack of Attachment

You'll notice with a gaslighting friend that the friendship is never fully reciprocated. There is no give and take. It's all take, all the time. While you may feel close to this person and would drop everything to bring her food were there a death in her family, for example, she wouldn't even call you if there were a death in yours. You would gladly help your gaslighting friend move into her new house, but when you need help moving, she's nowhere to be found. In a friendship with a gaslighter, you are doing all the giving, and your gaslighting friend is doing all the taking. This includes taking your time and energy until you are exhausted.

"I am always there for my neighbor, whatever she needs. But when I need something? Crickets."

—Yasmin, 35

Gaslighting friends blame you for not doing enough for them, or won't be there for you in your time of need—even when you have given and given until you can't give anymore. You are exhausted just from having this one person in your life. You must understand that you will never fulfill gaslighters' narcissistic needs. They are a bottomless pit.

Why do they do this? Gaslighters scurry away from healthy attachments to other relationships that they can control. They may act like your best friend today but will disappear if they find someone who seems "better," "more fun," or of higher social status. To gaslighters, it's all about appearance. Because of their "all or nothing" cognitive distortion, they can't manage having more than one friend at a time. Either Friend A is 100 percent wonderful

> "When my friend's mother died, I brought over food, offered to watch her kids—but when my dad died, I never heard from her. Never even texted, much less called."
>
> —*Sammy, 50*

and Friend B is 100 percent terrible, or vice versa. There is no middle ground. Gaslighters will leave you high and dry with no explanation. While you are searching online for answers or asking other friends what you did to make such people completely ignore you, the gaslighters have moved on to their next victim, their new "best friend." *They do not care.* They don't care about your feelings, and they don't care about the new friend's feelings. They lack the capacity. They have no ability to function as an empathic, decent human being.

The best thing to do is to stop expecting gaslighters to be something they are not. They never will be able to empathize with you, or keep a confidence. Neither will they be supportive in your time of need, or be understanding if you are unable to help them at a particular time.

They Don't Really Want a "Friend"

You'll notice that gaslighters don't want a friend as much as they want a pet. They're looking for "friends" who will be dependent on them and cater to their every whim. Gaslighters don't know how to form real friendships. You know a healthy friendship when you're in one, but let's take a closer look. A healthy friendship is based on:

> "A friend of mine was always sweet and giving—until one time I told her I didn't want to go shopping with her. It was like a monster took over. She sent me texts telling me what a bitch and loser I was."
>
> —*Daria, 25*

- Mutual respect
- Mutual admiration

- Being your authentic selves
- Sharing mutual interests
- Having similar values

You share a sense of what's important in life—love, commitment, caring, respect, diversity, and much more.

If you take a good look at your friendship with a gaslighter, you'll see that it does not meet your core values of love, respect, and caring. This is because gaslighters don't feel these things for other people. Remember, you can't change other people's values or how they treat you. If you find yourself in a "friendship" with a gaslighter, your only real choice is to end it.

Lack of Authenticity

Throughout this book, we've seen this quality of inauthenticity in gaslighters. They put on a show, acting the way they *think* they should act to get what they want. When you look at your most fulfilling friendships, I'm sure you notice that you can be yourself with these friends—there is no judgment. They accept you as you are and care about you as you are. As we've been seeing, this is not the case with gaslighters. Oh, they'll start out being friendly—and charming and even generous—but then turn on you quickly. The person you thought you knew was not real.

"I saw something kind of scary—a friend of mine, who was being cordial with guests at her party, turned around and it was like a mask fell off. Her facial expression completely changed to something I had never seen before—total rage. This was more than just 'I'm having a bad day and getting through this.'"

—Rose, 60

Gaslighters don't have a solid grip on who they are as people. They lack what psychologists call an "integrated personality." An integrated personality means that you have a good sense of who you are—you know your wants, your needs, and you have boundaries of what is healthy and unhealthy. Because of this lack of integrated personality, gaslighters lack the very capacity for being themselves with others—

they aren't sure what their "self" is like. When you try to be friends with gaslighters, things don't seem to be quite real; they seem put on or fake. Without this basic authenticity, a healthy, intimate friendship simply isn't possible.

"But I Don't Want to Lose a Friend"

One of the tricks that gaslighters pull is to manipulate you into being dependent on them. You may feel that your world will fall apart when you no longer have a particular person to lean on. But think back on your friendship. Was the gaslighter really ever there for you when you needed her? Or did she have excuses for why she couldn't help you, or listen to a concern?

You may be concerned that you will lose the friendship by setting boundaries with the gaslighter, and you probably will. The truth is, you never really had a friend in the gaslighter. What you saw was a carefully orchestrated act to make you think you did. But what I want you to know is this: Now that you know what to watch for and how to evaluate the health of your friendships, you are readier than ever to get out there and make new friends. Out of the billions of people in the world, there are plenty who would love to know you.

GASLIGHTING NEIGHBORS

At the beginning of this chapter we talked about how cutting ties with a gaslighting friend can be easier than cutting ties with a gaslighting family member. We get to choose our friends, however emotional and difficult it can be to navigate endings. But there are people in our lives aside from family members whom it's not so easy to get away from. Namely, neighbors. Sometimes we have the unfortunate burden of living next to a gaslighter. As you read earlier, gaslighters are really good at hiding their true dysfunctional selves. It may take a while to realize what's happening, but somehow the neighbor who was so sweet when you moved in has now become a nightmare.

If this sounds familiar, if you think your neighbor is a gaslighter, here are a few key tips: Do not disclose personal information to him or her. Also, do not entertain unwanted visits. Request that your neighbor call before stopping by. Be friendly but firm. Also, just because someone is at your door doesn't mean you have to open it.

Gaslighting neighbors have all kinds of ways of haunting our lives. They may:

- Infringe on your property line
- Blatantly violate building codes
- Be verbally aggressive when you walk by
- Get in your personal space
- Spread rumors in the neighborhood about you
- Ask for favors and get angry if you say no
- Not understand why you've distanced yourself from them
- Get irrationally angry if your dog urinates in their yard
- Try to lure your pets over to their yard
- Try to poison your pets
- Invite you to gossip about other neighbors
- Ask you repeatedly about unpleasant events in your life
- Tell you about a neighbor that supposedly has said unflattering things about you
- Call the police if they feel you are being too loud and on and on.

"My neighbor put aluminum foil on the outside of a window facing our house because I had told him that his floodlights were streaming right into our bedroom. Now I get the floodlights at night and blinding sunlight in the morning."

—James, 45

Keep in mind that most neighbors are not gaslighters. However, if you have one, arm yourself with information or they can turn your once-peaceful home into a living hell.

Get to know your city's code enforcement rules. Do what is called "keeping your side of the street clean"—follow your neighborhood's rules and laws to a T. Chances are, your gaslighting neighbor is watching you like a hawk and waiting for the moment you do something that violates city code, no matter how small the infraction.

Gaslighters are more likely to turn you in if they are constant code violators themselves. This is because gaslighters always accuse people of doing what they are doing themselves—they think they don't need to follow the same rules everyone else has to follow. Gaslighters are well known for violating city codes. They love to get even with people, even if it is just in their own mind. Make sure you are following these standard "good citizen" rules:

> "My neighbor yelled at me because my dog was peeing on the strip of grass between the sidewalk and the street. It's not even her property."
>
> —Jacqueline, 55

- Be meticulous about picking up after your dog.
- Never let your dog off-leash.
- Be knowledgeable of city noise ordinances and follow them.
- Don't operate loud yard equipment before eight a.m. on a weekday and nine a.m. on a weekend.

To protect yourself, consider doing the following:

- Record the actual noise volume at your parties. Noise violations are often among the first things gaslighters will zero in on.
- Do not so much as step on your neighbor's property.
- Keep documentation. As you learned from Chapter 4 on gaslighters in the workplace, it is important to keep legal documentation if you need to consult with an attorney. Record time, date, and direct quotes from your interactions.
- If your gaslighting neighbor is infringing on your property, try installing security cameras you can run from your laptop or tablet. They are becoming more and more affordable.
- Consult with an attorney.

Stay as far away from your neighbor as possible. This may be difficult if your gaslighting neighbor lives next door, but if they live down at the end of your street, walk or drive by the gaslighter's house as little as possible. Yes, it may present an inconvenience to you, but it is better to have an inconvenience than stir up trouble with the gaslighter. The gaslighter would have no qualms about telling the police you did something unlawful as you were walking or driving by his house. All it takes is another neighbor to corroborate that you were seen in that area at that time, or a lying neighbor who was intimidated or blackmailed by the gaslighter. This witness doesn't even have to have seen you do anything—just the fact that they can confirm you were in the area will make life much more difficult for you.

"Our dog ran out the front door. We got him right back inside. But my neighbor called animal control, saying we were irresponsible owners. He looks for anything he can turn us in for."

—Maude, 30

Tell your kids to avoid going near your neighbor's house. If your kids ask why, just say that it's a new rule you have now. If you tell your kids "Because Mr. X is not a nice person," that will get back to Mr. X—guaranteed. No need to stir things up even more.

If you have outdoor pets, it is also very important that your pet not get into your neighbor's yard, whether through a breach in the fence or by escaping out the front door. If your pet gets into the neighbor's yard, a gaslighter may call animal control, or worse, shoot or poison the animal. Believe me, I've heard stories that would break your heart. Don't walk your dog past the neighbor's house. This sounds extreme, but remember, when you are dealing with a gaslighter, you are dealing with a very unstable and angry person.

Limit contact with your neighbor as much as possible. If you see her at a neighborhood event, act as if she is not there, or excuse yourself. Try to avoid eye contact—the gaslighter will see direct eye contact as a challenge. Many people think that by not making eye contact or talking to a gaslighter, you are somehow "allowing" the gaslighter to continue behaving badly. What you are doing is refraining from provoking the gaslighter into more unstable behavior. Remember, gaslighters do not operate like regular people. Ignoring them or leaving the situation really is the best policy.

You may get to the point where you don't even want to attend neighborhood get-togethers if you know the gaslighter is going to be there. In time, your neighbors will see the kind of person the gaslighter is, and the gaslighter will be invited to fewer and fewer get-togethers anyway. The gaslighter can only keep up his facade for so long.

Court dockets are filled with cases of neighbors behaving very badly, and restraining orders, in which a judge orders the person to stay a certain distance from you for a defined period of time, are often the only remedy available, however imperfect.

There are cases of a neighbor tormenting a family to the point where the family was granted a restraining order. In one well-publicized case, a woman was actually barred from entering her neighborhood due to the harassment she was dishing out to her neighbors.

In these sorts of cases, gaslighters/defendants view themselves as the wronged one. They mounted their campaigns of revenge, claiming they had legitimate reasons to harass their neighbors. They feel they are justified in doing "whatever it takes" to make the other person "pay," even if it results in the gaslighters' being hit with restraining orders, jail time, or probation.

Sometimes the courts are our best or only protection against a gaslighter, but it's rarely easy street. A restraining order must be approved by a judge, and it states that a person may not initiate contact with you and must stay a certain distance from you at all times. You may qualify for a restraining order if a person poses an imminent or immediate threat to you or your family. For more on restraining orders, see the Resources section at the end of this book.

GASLIGHTING LANDLORDS

There's one more category of gaslighters to look at here before we turn to our next chapter: your landlord. You know the type. He never fixed your plumbing but he says he did. He claims to have had conversations with you that never actually happened. He comes around when you haven't contacted him, just to see "how you're doing." If you have the unfortunate experience of being stalked or harassed by a landlord, know that there are legal remedies or solutions. First, know your state's tenant laws. In many states, your landlord has to have a very valid reason for coming around unannounced, or he is breaking the law. If this is the case in your state, tell your landlord that he needs to notify you at least 24 hours before appearing at your home. Better yet, have it added as a clause in your lease. If he appears again without notice, contact local law enforcement. Keep documentation of all interactions with your landlord. You can also expect that your gaslighting landlord will try to keep your security deposit. Remember how cheap gaslighters are? He'll make up a reason but the real reason, other than cheapness, is to get revenge on you. Before you move out, make sure your house or apartment is thoroughly cleaned. Take photos of everything, even under the kitchen and bathroom sinks. If your landlord keeps your security deposit without cause, you can take him to small claims court and recover it. But you'll need documentation. Also, please seek the advice of an attorney if you are considering legal action. Local tenants unions and/or rent boards can help you navigate.

WHAT TO DO ABOUT GASLIGHTING FRIENDS AND NEIGHBORS

Whether the gaslighter is a friend or neighbor, there are ways to protect yourself. These options include cutting off contact, distancing yourself, avoiding borrowing anything from or giving anything to the gaslighter, and seeking legal representation for yourself.

Stay Away from Them or Cut Off Contact

If the gaslighter is a friend, your best bet, hard as it may be, is to cut all ties with them. This is usually the only way to get rid of the toxic influence of a gaslighter. If you are on a social committee with them, at your child's school, for instance, transfer to another one. If you don't, this person will continue to wreak havoc in your life—guaranteed. There is a small chance that the gaslighter will become preoccupied with someone else and drop you like a hot potato, but until then she will likely make your life drama filled.

If you have a gaslighting neighbor who is continually harassing you, you might want to consider moving. Yes, seriously. While that is a big adjustment to make and may wind up costing you money and time, it might well be worth it for peace of mind. Moving out may feel like giving in or like the gaslighter has "won," but believe me, *you* have won by putting your family's well-being first.

Never Give Anything to or Borrow Anything from a Gaslighter

Never loan anything to a gaslighter. If you do loan something, do it with the expectation that you will never get it back. And never, under any circumstances, should you loan the gaslighter money. Likewise, never borrow

> "I don't let certain people 'borrow' things unless I am willing to part with it for good."
>
> —Declan, 35

anything from a gaslighter. The gaslighter will conveniently "forget" that you borrowed an item, and will then accuse you of stealing it.

If the gaslighter gives you an item as a "gift," either say "No, thank you" or, if you really must take it, be aware that it may come back to bite you. Gaslighters are famous for "gifting" you something, then claiming that you stole it from them. Again, this is all about feeling the need to get even with people who they feel have wronged them. It can also stem from their substance abuse. Remember that gaslighters may have more problems with addiction than the rest of us do, and they may have given you something while in a blackout.

> "Sometimes a gift from a 'friend' is an invitation to trouble. The gifts are never 'free'—they come with a lot of hassle."
>
> —Evie, 39

Never Have Gaslighters Take Care of Your Children or Pets

It's never a good idea to have gaslighters take care of your children or pets. They will turn your children against you. They will "forget" about your child's food allergies, or the rules you have in your home. Your pets will be neglected or abused. They will be fed things you expressly told the gaslighter not to give them. Gaslighters don't care. If you give them the responsibility of watching your children or your pets, they'll take that as carte blanche, putting themselves in a position of power over the most valuable beings in your life. Please don't rationalize that you don't have anyone else to watch your child or pet. There's got to be a better option than leaving them with a gaslighter who may cause them serious harm.

Act Bored or Ambivalent

The best way to end a friendship with a gaslighter is to have the gaslighter get tired of you and walk away first. As we've seen again and again, gaslighters love to get people stirred up. If you respond to gaslighters' inflammatory remarks with "that might be true," "okay," and "maybe," they will soon become bored with you. If you act ambivalent or bored and fail to let them get a rise out of you, they will quickly move on. What you don't want to do, even if it seems more honest or decent, is say, "We can't hang out anymore." That will only bring on their rage. One thing you can be sure of is that gaslighters have a deep-seated fear of abandonment and loss of control. Remember, no matter how bad you may feel about their troubles, you can't fix them. Your only healthy option is to get away.

State the Obvious and Seek Legal Remedies

If you have set limits and the gaslighter still won't leave you or your family alone, let him know clearly that he's not welcome at your home. If you have set limits and the gaslighter still goes onto your property, he's trespassing. Contact your local law enforcement agency for instances of trespassing, stalking, or if the gaslighter threatens you or your family. Contact an attorney if the gaslighter has ramped up his behavior to this point. You may need to file a restraining order. As noted earlier, a restraining order must be approved by a judge, and it states that a person may not initiate contact with you, and they must stay a certain distance from you at all times. You may qualify for a restraining order if a person poses an imminent or immediate threat to you or your family. It is critical that you keep documentation of how the person has harassed or threatened you.

If the gaslighter posts threatening or false information about you or your business on the Internet, including social media, take screenshots and report the incident(s) to the site. Contact an attorney about possibly issuing a "cease and desist" order to prevent the gaslighter from further harassing you.

There are two legal terms for this kind of harassment: *libel* and *slander*. Libel is when someone prints something about you that is both false and damaging to you. Slander is when someone says something that is both false and damaging to you. Suing someone for libel or slander is tricky—you have to prove that you or your business suffered directly from this person's false statements—but it can be done. See an attorney for more information.

GASLIGHTING FRIENDS ARE not really friends at all. They aren't looking out for your best interests, nor can they really form healthy relationships. And just as with gaslighting friends, gaslighting neighbors and landlords can lack boundaries. It is up to you to put those boundaries in place—whether it is scaling back on your involvement, telling gaslighters that their behavior isn't acceptable, getting legal advice or interventions, or cutting off contact completely. The option you choose depends on your relationship with the gaslighters and whether logistically you can truly get away from them.

Getting away from a gaslighting friend and healing yourself can be a challenge. For more information on counseling and other ways to heal from your relationship with a gaslighter, see Chapter 12. In the next chapter, you'll learn how to navigate through divorcing and also coparenting with a gaslighter.

10

YOUR EX, YOUR KIDS, YOUR EX'S NEW SPOUSE, YOUR NEW SPOUSE'S EX

Gaslighting in Divorce and Coparenting

PERHAPS THIS BOOK HAS GIVEN YOU THE COURAGE TO LEAVE A gaslighting spouse, or maybe that process was already under way when you found your way here. In either case, leaving a gaslighter puts you into very tricky territory. With everything you've learned so far about how gaslighters tend to operate, it's not hard to see that divorcing, and then coparenting with, one can be a harrowing and tortuous process. Gaslighters will always find a way to kick you when you're down, making the pain of your divorce even worse. If you have kids together, seeing them being impacted by the gaslighter's behavior can bring out or intensify your feelings of anger and hatred toward your former spouse. But it certainly can be done. You can—you must—leave the gaslighter to get on with your life. I'm going to show you how. And if you've already left, this chapter can give you some good guidance for how to continue coparenting with a gaslighter (or what to do if your ex marries one or your new spouse brings a gaslighting ex into the picture).

DIVORCING A GASLIGHTER

I realize that the information in this chapter may make you feel pretty powerless. You want to protect yourself and your child, and with gaslighters that can sometimes seem impossible. But there are steps you can and should take to make the process go as smoothly as possible if you are divorcing a gaslighter or working out coparenting with one. Expect some level of conflict but know that you are doing the right thing to get away. And being separated or divorced from the gaslighter usually gives you more space to detach and get some needed perspective.

All divorces involving a gaslighter would fall into the category of "high-conflict divorce." Knowing what makes up a high-conflict divorce helps you know what to expect during a divorce from a gaslighter, and also helps you identify what you might be going through. This leads to you feeling more in control of your situation. High-conflict divorces are ones in which either or both partners:

- Get into a fight almost every time they meet
- Have a Cluster B personality disorder (antisocial, borderline, histrionic, or narcissistic)
- Have a history of domestic violence
- Have had involvement from social services regarding child welfare
- Have a history of violent crime
- Refuse to comply with judicial orders
- Sabotage communications between the parties
- Sabotage communication between the other parent and the children
- Cause conflict during child exchange
- Have a restraining order against them

Hire an Attorney

Divorce is never an easy process, even when both parties are civil to each other. When you are divorcing a gaslighter, it can be a wild, unpredictable ride. You need a family law attorney who has expertise in working in high-conflict divorces, and also who wants the process to be done as fairly and equitably as possible. If you have financial hardship, there are family law attorneys who are willing to work *pro bono* (at no charge) or *low bono* (for a nominal fee), particularly in cases of domestic abuse. See the Resources section at the end of this book for more information.

Family law attorneys specialize in cases of marriage, divorce, parenting, adoption, surrogacy, and juvenile law-breaking. You can find the right attorney for you by getting referrals from your community, reading reviews online, and then directly contacting the attorney.

When you first meet with an attorney, ask how much she charges and how much experience she has with high-conflict divorces. Let her know that your ex is very manipulative. During this discussion, pay attention to whether you feel comfortable sharing this information with your attorney. Does it seem that this attorney is knowledgeable about how to handle manipulative exes? Did the attorney or her receptionist return your call in a reasonable amount of time? If not, consider that a red flag. You need someone who recognizes the seriousness of your situation. You may need to interview a few attorneys before you meet the one that is best for you. Make sure you choose an attorney with whom you feel comfortable asking questions—your and your children's well-being is at stake.

Once you have hired an attorney, bring along documentation for the issues you have had with your ex. This can be in the form of a note-taking app, a notebook, or any other organized form of writing (e-mails, texts with your ex, etc.). You can also include videos or recordings of phone calls, but be aware of your state laws regarding the recording of others.

Mediation

In some states, when you are divorcing you are required to go to mediation first, instead of going directly to court. (An exception to this is if your attorney feels that mediation will not result in the best outcome for you and your children, and recommends that you have a judge make decisions about your case.) A mediator is a trained, neutral third party who helps you and your spouse come to an agreement regarding marital assets (property, such as furniture and a house); scheduled time with children; how the parents will share decision-making power (the most common option is that both exes have decision-making power) for children's medical and school issues; child support amounts; and who pays for afterschool activities and/or daycare. If you are divorcing pro se (without attorney representation), just the two of you will meet with the mediator. If you are represented by an attorney, she will meet you at the mediator's office or you will go there together. The mediator may even come to you in some cases.

> "My ex has been abusive, so I told the mediator that I felt unsafe around him. She did mediation in a way that I never even saw my ex, and I left her office way before he did."
>
> —Julianne, 30

If you feel unsafe meeting directly with your soon-to-be-ex in mediation, let the mediator know ahead of time. When speaking with the mediator, let him know that your spouse has been volatile in the past, and you are concerned for your safety. Let him know that you are open to mediation, but you do not want to be in the same room with your spouse under any circumstance. Tell the mediator you want to leave his office before your soon-to-be-ex arrives.

> "Mediation was a good way to keep our focus on what was best for our kids."
>
> —Lisi, 34

Collaborative Divorce

There is something called a collaborative divorce. This can be an ideal way to work through a divorce with a gaslighter. In a collaborative divorce, you meet as a team to divorce in a way that helps you, your spouse, and your children have the calmest transition possible. In a collaborative team meeting, a facilitator (usually a mental health professional) leads the team. The facilitator is a neutral party there to help the meeting run smoothly. The rest of the collaborative team consists of you, your ex, your attorney, your ex's attorney, and a financial representative. The benefits of the collaborative divorce are that everyone on the team is working toward the best interests of you, your ex, and your children. In collaborative divorce, you focus on shared goals, such as the happiness and safety of your children.

> "Collaborative divorce helped my ex and me with stuff we would always have fought about before. When things were getting heated, the man running the meeting reminded us that we were divorcing this way because we wanted our kids to be happy."
>
> —Julio, 38

Because the team is all working together, there is less of a chance of your gaslighting spouse "playing" the members of the team against one another. If the facilitator is on his game and the team is cohesive, he and the other team members will spot this and put the gaslighter's manipulation to a grinding halt. Collaborative divorce can be more expensive than standard divorce, given all the players involved who need to be paid. However, since your divorce process may be more efficient and less traumatic, it may actually cost you less money than in a "standard" divorce process. Again, a discussion with your attorney can help you decide whether the collaborative route is the way to go in your case.

> "I felt really comfortable and safe in the collaborative process, even though divorce is a difficult thing to go through. The team members helped us stay on track and focus on the most important thing—the well-being of our kids."
>
> —Francesca, 38

THE SAGA CONTINUES: COPARENTING AFTER LEAVING A GASLIGHTER

Making the decision to divorce a gaslighter is one of the toughest and courageous things you can do, and if you have children with this person, it can be terribly disheartening to realize you can never truly be free of him. How do you balance protecting your kids with not making the situation with the gaslighter worse? How do you coparent with someone who doesn't have you or your children's best interests in mind? How do you coexist alongside someone who lives to make your life miserable?

You may be realizing how much your and your children's quality of life has been impacted by his crazy-making behavior—it's hard to keep track of all the manipulation tactics and lies when you are coparenting with a gaslighter—and yet you can't deny your children a relationship with their other parent. However, there is hope for you and your children to have a bright future.

It is important to recognize what tricks your gaslighter is likely to use to keep you under his grip, as well as the tricks he's likely to use to try to pit your children against you or otherwise weaponize them against you. I'll teach you how to coparent to the best of your ability even when your coparenting partner is constantly trying to undermine you. I'll give you the best information I have on how to protect yourself and your children from the damage of a gaslighter.

Traits of Gaslighting Parents

Gaslighting parents tend to:

- Alienate their children from the other parent
- Not return the children to the other parent at the agreed-upon time
- Change plans at the last minute regarding time with the children
- Speak badly about the other parent, with the children present
- Not show up for scheduled pickup and drop-off
- Disappear from the children's life entirely
- Refuse to pay child support or spousal support, as ordered by the court
- Act abusively toward the children
- Talk, or relay messages, to the other parent through the children
- Prevent the children from speaking to the other parent
- Tell the children that they can't do an activity because the other parent is "taking all my money"

- Make the children call a new partner "Mom" or "Dad"
- Have the children snoop on the other parent and report back to them
- Fail to show up to court-ordered mediation
- Fail to practice "right of first refusal" with the other parent
- Leave paperwork about the separation, divorce, or parenting plan in clear view of the children

Later in this chapter, we'll look at what special considerations you should make when entering a high-conflict divorce.

Gaslighters Try to Poison Your Children Against You

It's common for a gaslighting parent to try to use your kids against you and drive a wedge in your relationship with your kids. It is a form of emotional abuse. This type of abuse can take years to heal from, and it can impact your child's relationship with you even into adulthood. That's why it's so important that you learn to spot the signs and have good tools for putting a stop to it.

In a divorce, gaslighters may become obsessed with feeling that they "won." They will often get irrationally jealous when you start dating again. Remember, gaslighters don't see people as people but as possessions. If your ex feels he has been "wronged," he may try to make your life difficult. Add kids to this combustible situation and the gaslighter will usually make a concerted effort to portray you to your kids as the "bad parent" so as to "win" their favor.

> "My ex told my son that my boyfriend was a drug dealer and that I slept around. Surprise, surprise, my son started refusing to come home. None of what my ex said was true. I wound up taking him to court, and the judge said my ex was a bad influence on my son. My ex didn't care that what he said was a lie, and that it was hurting our son—he just wanted to 'win.'"
>
> —Janet, 38

Tragically and confusingly for your kids, this has nothing to do with the gaslighting parent actually wanting or loving your child; it's about hurting you where you are most vulnerable—in your relationship with your children. Gaslighters have to "win" and so they need you to "lose," at all costs—even if it destroys your children psychologically.

I have seen this too often, and there are too many stories out there to count.

In one particular custody case, the father petitioned for primary custody of his son, claiming that the mother was an unfit parent. The son had begun spending a majority of his after-school time with the father instead of the mother, going against the parenting plan. The father had a history of not returning the son to the mother on time, degraded the mother in front of the son, left sexually explicit material in view of the son, and encouraged the son to defy the mother's rules. In addition, the son's grades had dropped since he'd started spending so much time at his father's house. The court found no evidence that the mother was an unfit parent, and ruled that the son's statements about wanting to live with the father were "coached," meaning that they sounded rehearsed and as if he was repeating what his father had told him to say. The visitation agreement as written was ordered to be enforced, with the father going back to seeing the son every other weekend and one day a week.

In another custody case, the mother would video record the exchange of her child with the father at a mutually agreed-upon location. She presented the recordings as evidence that the child did not want to go with the father and that she should get full custody. Recording the exchanges actually worked against the mother—they showed her encouraging the child to stay with her and not get into the father's car. This included the mother's "reminding" the child why he didn't want to go with the father. Remarkably, the recordings also showed the mother promising the child special trips and gifts if he stayed with her and didn't go with the father. The gaslighting mother must not have even considered how badly these recordings made her look! Primary custody was denied, and shared custody continued as per the agreement, with mandatory counseling for the mother.

> "My ex was pretty quiet until he found out from my sister that I was dating. All of the sudden he started showing up late to exchanges, with no text, phone call, or explanation. He started refusing to talk to me about our son's schedule, his soccer practice, pretty much everything."
>
> —Courtney, 31

In these cases, you see how easily a gaslighter ex can influence a child or children against the other parent. Gaslighters are notorious for telling their children that the other parent is bad or not worthy of them. They shower the child with gifts and special trips, tell the child that the other parent's rules are ridiculous and strict, let the child stay up late, tell the child that they don't have to show up on time to the exchange point—all things that greatly influence children.

Teenagers are especially susceptible to this type of influence, because of their inherent rebelliousness. During a developmental stage where parents need to set clear boundaries, the gaslighting parent appears to let the teen have free rein. What teenager wouldn't be tempted by that?

Granted, there is a flip side to coparenting with a gaslighter. Gaslighters who have immediately found a new partner may "forget" their children. The gaslighting parent is now nowhere to be found. Child support is garnished from his paychecks because he can't be bothered to uphold his obligations or be a participant in his child's life. This is another way that gaslighters punish—by putting the complete parenting responsibility on their former spouse.

We have already discussed how gaslighters can harm their children, in Chapter 8. If you refer back to that chapter, you will also find a list of warning signs that your children have started using the gaslighting parent's manipulation tactics. By knowing these warning signs, you can stay one step ahead and make sure your children get the help they need to be happy and healthy—including counseling, being surrounded by positive role models, and having a strong, healthy relationship with you.

The good news is that there is hope for you and your children. In many cases, gaslighters get the help *they* need (or are court-ordered to get) and they become less of an issue over time. You also have more support available than you realize—from friends, family, professionals, and your community. The most important thing is to keep being the best parent you can be. You may want to look into counseling for yourself and your kids; the end of this chapter as well as Chapter 12 offer more information.

Increased Chances of Child Abuse

All gaslighting parents see their children as extensions of themselves, but when the other parent isn't present as a moderating influence, the possibilities for abuse escalate, especially during periods—toddlerhood, the preteen years—when a child should be individuating from the parent. During individuation, children start saying no more often and start testing boundaries with you. This is developmentally normal. Your children are exercising their freedom and want to know the boundaries of this freedom.

Psychologically healthy parents will want their children to learn how to function on their own in the world. They'll see this separating as normal. Gaslighters, by contrast, will look upon their children's individuation with rage and disgust, viewing that independence as a form of abandonment and betrayal. Gaslighters know that when children are independent, they have less control over them. They will do whatever is in their power to stop those children from being their own person—and this can easily lead to abuse.

If you feel your child may be being abused, contact your local law enforcement or your state's abuse hotline. For more information, see the Resources section at the end of this book. Of course if you think your child is being abused, it will be excruciatingly hard not to lash out at the gaslighter. Don't do it. I cannot possibly overstate this. Do not lash out. You need to be available for your child, even more than ever, and it's very difficult to do that if your ex files a court order against you or you go so far as to be in police custody or prison. Instead, get yourself and your children into counseling immediately. Also speak with a family law attorney about you and your child's rights, including filing an emergency motion regarding custody and visitation.

REFUSE TO ARGUE WITH THE GASLIGHTER

In general, you want to avoid arguing with gaslighters. Just talk about facts and try to avoid using your emotions. I know this can be very difficult to do, but becoming emotional with gaslighters gives them the reward they're looking for. They thrive on knowing they've gotten under your skin, and they'll just jack up the manipulative behavior if they think they're succeeding. It's all a game with them, and you will never win an argument with a gaslighter. It's like arguing with someone who is drunk. The best thing you can do is maintain a calm voice, even if you feel as though you are going to explode inside.

> "I was constantly falling for my ex's snide comments and getting into fights with her on the phone. Finally I realized that when we were fighting, I was still having some emotional interaction with her. With a therapist's help, I learned how gaslighters work hard at getting people upset. That really helped me heal, and made me realize I wasn't the crazy one."
>
> —Jerusha, 35

Remember, gaslighters feed off your anger and frustration. Do not give them that power. When they don't get a reaction out of you, they may start upping the ante, or increasing their damaging behaviors. This does not mean you need to tolerate yelling or verbal abuse, however. If your ex starts yelling at you or calling you names over the phone, calmly hang up.

If you are receiving verbal abuse via text, take screen shots and do not respond to the texts. Just as when you argue over the phone, by responding you are giving gaslighters the rise they're looking for. If you show you are riled up, you are rewarding the behavior that you want to stop. I know how hard holding back can be to do.

If gaslighters try to anger you, I recommend that you pause for a deep breath to a count of three. This sounds so simple, but you'll be amazed at how it can help you regain composure and communicate—or terminate the conversation, as need be—without emotion.

What's in It for You?

If you find yourself being pulled into an argument with your gaslighting ex, look into why that is happening. Your ex probably knows your most vulnerable spots, such as some insecurities you may have about how you parent your kids. The gaslighter will go right after those soft spots to provoke you into lashing out and looking unstable. You can't afford this, and no good will come of it. Not arguing means little to no contact.

I encourage you to ask yourself what's in it for you. Could it be that you are engaging in fighting with your ex because it means you can still have some attachment to him? It can be very difficult to break that attachment. This person manipulated you in a way that made you feel dependent on him, and then he abused your trust. It can be very difficult to cope with that.

If you think you fight with your ex because you still crave some attachment to him, take a step back and examine why. Do you feel a sense of excitement when you fight with him? Does it seem as though your ex knows exactly what to say to upset you? Going to counseling can be really helpful in stopping this pattern of fighting just to stay close.

"Every single time we talk on the phone, there's an argument. I told her texting and e-mail would be best. This way we argue less, and I have documentation of what was said. No more 'I told you to pick the kids up at 6' when it was clearly 7."

—Jorge, 41

I'd also encourage you to think about how your arguing might be affecting your children's well-being, including their emotional health. They are probably more aware of the fighting with your ex than you realize. Are they around when you take your ex's phone calls? Respond to his texts? Kids are very perceptive about friction like this, even if it's just over texts, and it can start to affect their mood, sleep, appetite, academic performance, and how they get along with you and their siblings. You may even notice that your children are showing physical signs of anxiety, such as biting their nails or pulling at their hair.

It is up to you to stop the pattern of fighting with a gaslighter ex. Gaslighters can't have an argument if you don't participate. If your ex says something rude, remember, you can always say, calmly, "I'm hanging up now," and do it. If you have children with your ex, you can consult with what's called a parent coordinator, to help improve communication with your ex. Later in this chapter you'll learn how these parent coordinators can help in high-conflict coparenting situations.

Consider just communicating with your ex via text or e-mails, where you can control whether and how to respond—and have a record of the exchange. There are even apps that will do the scheduling for you so you don't have to talk directly to your ex. See the Resources section at the end of this book for more information.

WHEN YOUR SPOUSE'S EX IS A GASLIGHTER

And what if you married someone with a gaslighting ex? Maybe you were aware that your spouse's ex had issues before you got married, or maybe it was only later that you were welcomed into the inner sanctum of the ex's insanity. Here are a few words to live by: You are not responsible for your spouse's ex's behavior (or your spouse's behavior, for that matter). You did nothing wrong by marrying your spouse, even if the gaslighting ex is trying to punish you for it. If you got together with your spouse via an affair, it's understandable that his ex-spouse would be upset. But there is a big difference between being upset and stalking and harassing, as gaslighters tend to do. In a moment, we'll look at how to set good boundaries with your spouse's gaslighting ex.

STEPPARENTING

If your spouse has kids with his ex, the challenges of course multiply. Being a stepparent is tough enough when there isn't a gaslighter in the picture—you get all the responsibilities of being a parent with none of the ability to provide guidance or limit-setting. However, what you *can* set are your own limits as to how you will be treated. If your spouse's ex is a gaslighter, it is important that your spouse be on board with your boundaries with his kids. Good boundaries with your stepchildren include their speaking to you in a calm tone, and staying out of your personal belongings (a gaslighting parent will often recruit a child on a "search and find" mission). Likewise, you must do the same for them. Be very careful about not disciplining your stepchildren. That is not your job or your role—that is up to

> "My husband's ex cornered me one day and told me what we had eaten for dinner every day that week. It was very creepy. My guess is that she was just letting me know that my stepson was sharing information with her, and that she was in control."
>
> —Janie, 35

your spouse and the children's other parent. If you do discipline the children, the gaslighter will be all over you. Avoid a potential blow-up by not trying to parent her children. Have a clear set of guidelines for the stepchildren's behavior at home. Post these rules in a visible location, such as the refrigerator door. This eliminates quite a bit of arguments between stepparent and spouse.

It is very important that you and your spouse come to agreement on boundaries with his ex and their children. You should not tolerate your partner's ex:

- Getting in your personal space
- Telling your stepchildren lies about you
- Sabotaging your relationship with your stepchildren
- Encouraging your stepchildren to snoop on you
- Showing up at your house without contacting you first
- Showing up at your workplace

In cases such as these, you may benefit from having you, your spouse, and your spouse's ex discuss these boundary violations in counseling sessions. If this reaffirming and creation of healthy boundaries is not enough, consult with an attorney.

Many times, people will marry a person with children with the unconscious wish to "save" or "fix" the family. This Florence Nightingale fantasy can be especially appealing when the spouse's ex is a gaslighter and has done psychological damage to the family; you think you can be a good influence for these "poor kids." Tricky, tricky territory, especially when the family you marry into doesn't realize the severity of the other parent's pathology. Your spouse's ex's whirlwind of destructive behavior is "normal" to them, and having you point out the gaslighting behaviors is likely to cause some explosions.

"My stepson blatantly went against rules when it was just he and I at home. It turns out his mother was encouraging him to cause trouble for me."

—Lauren, 30

If your spouse still has an emotional attachment to the gaslighter, she may not want to hear what you have to say and will blame you for bringing it up. She may accuse you of jealousy or think you're trying to drive some sort of wedge between the exes. If you find yourself in this situation, it may be time for couples counseling, or you may need to reevaluate your standing with your spouse and consider whether it is time to leave the relationship. Remember, you can't make anyone do anything, including making your spouse realize that her ex's behavior is not acceptable.

SHOULD YOU TELL YOUR CHILDREN THEIR PARENT IS A GASLIGHTER?

If you are the one with the gaslighting ex, it can be a special challenge to talk with your kids about their other parent's behavior. One of the most difficult parts of having a gaslighting ex is seeing how your kids suffer due to the gaslighter's behavior. It is a thin line between commiserating with them and expecting children to take your side against their other parent; for instance, "Your mom didn't pick you up because she's not a reliable person." Please, please refrain from saying negative things about your ex to your children, no matter how tempting. You are doing no one a favor. What you tell your children will get back to the gaslighter eventually, and the gaslighter will then use that against you. Instead, vent your frustrations with your friends and with a mental health professional. Your children are not an appropriate forum.

The gaslighter, as terrible as he may be, is still your child's parent. Children have a love for their parent that goes far beyond logic and understanding. It's similar to the love you have for your children—you love them beyond reason. Also, your children's love for their other parent is completely different from the love you once had for that person. The children's love is unconditional. Chances are, if you tell your children that their other parent is a gaslighter, they will get upset with you for maligning him. It's a road you don't want to go down.

You may feel that you have to be the "bad guy" almost all of the time, while the gaslighting parent gets to be the "fun parent." You might wish you could tell your children about the true nature of their other parent. Here's what usually happens when you give in to that urge to tell the "truth." First, this information will get back to the gaslighter. Guaranteed. The gaslighter will either pump your children for this information or bribe them with gifts or special privileges. Or, if you are speaking negatively about their other parent, the children will tell that parent because they are sure what you said about that parent is wrong. Put yourself in your kids' shoes. What good could come from knowing what you really think of their other mom or dad?

Your kids may also simply volunteer this information because it is the nature of children both to tell the truth and to push your buttons. They also know how to self-preserve. If your child has broken a rule in the other parent's home, what better way to divert from his behavior than to offer to the other parent, "Guess what Mommy said about you?" This revelation will only serve to send the gaslighter into a white hot rage. The rage will not only be let out on you but possibly also your child.

BEST PRACTICES FOR COPARENTING WITH A GASLIGHTER

One of my hopes in including this chapter in the book is to pass along some of the wisdom and experiences of other parents who have separated from a gaslighter. Here is my list of best practices:

Have a Detailed Parenting Plan

A parenting plan is a detailed agreement between you and the other parent.

Parenting plans detail—perhaps child by child, as appropriate:

- Who will have the children on what holidays, and what is the time of drop-off and pick-up

- Where the children will attend school, and who will transport the children on which days
- Who is okay to watch the children when the children are at a parent's home
- Right of first refusal, where one parent must let the other parent know if he or she will be away longer than an agreed-upon time and give the other parent the right to have that time with the children instead of a babysitter
- How medical decisions should be made: will they be a joint decision between parents, or do the parents agree that one parent will make the final decision if an agreement can't be reached?
- Who will provide insurance coverage for the children and who will pay for it
- The amount of child support. This is usually determined by a formula according to state, and according to income and number of children. It is also determined by number of overnight visits. (If a noncustodial parent agrees to a certain number of overnight visits during the year, the amount of child support that person is responsible for may decrease.)
- What days each parent will have the children at his or her home
- The times and locations of exchanges between parents
- How the children can communicate with one parent when in the other parent's custody (text, e-mail, phone, video conferencing)
- At what times the children will have communications with one parent when in the other parents' custody
- Agreements about open communication between the parents
- The method in which the parents will communicate about scheduling and decision making—text, phone, e-mail, or videoconferencing
- Agreement that the children will never be asked or expected to call a parent's partner "Mom" or "Dad"
- How much notice one parent needs to give the other if the other parent wants to take the children on vacation (and who will pay for the passport if the travel is international)

- The terms under which a parent can take a child out of the country (usually the parent coordinator will have you abide by the Hague Convention, which lists countries with strict regulations on the returning of children reported as abducted by a parent)
- The time frame in which itineraries for children's travel must be furnished
- The notification process if one parent wants to move a certain number of miles away from the other parent. Distances of 50 miles or more are usually discussed in the presence of a parent coordinator or mediator.
- Where children will be exchanged, and the amount of time a parent must wait for the other parent to show before heading back home

This may all look tedious, but having a written plan, signed by you and the other parent, really helps reduce conflict. The more specific your parenting plan, the better. You want the parenting plan written in such a way that if there is any conflict with the other parent, the solution is right there in the plan. If you or the other parent has issues with something in the parenting plan at some point, the two of you can always consult your attorneys or your parent coordinator.

If you both agree to a change in the plan—let's say you now need to have Johnny at your house on Wednesday instead of Thursday—get this change in writing. For most parents, a simple verbal agreement is enough. However, with a gaslighter, you need documentation for everything.

Items to Include in a Parenting Plan

I recommend including the following items in your parenting plan. As always, consult with your attorney for the best course of action.

Exchange of Children in a Neutral Location: Pick up and drop off your children in a neutral location. A neutral location is one that has no emotional ties to either you, the other parent, or your children. Some parents pick a public location that is a halfway point between their homes. A public location is important, because people tend to be on better behavior when there are others around. A public location also means you have witnesses if a conflict happens with the other parent; it also means quicker access to law enforcement or emergency services if needed.

Who Is Allowed at Exchange Points: If your divorce is so high-conflict that being around the other parent is bound to cause problems, you can agree with the other parent to have family members or family friends bring your child to the exchange point. You can also have it added that only you or the other parent will be at the exchange point, as to avoid confrontations with former in-laws or new romantic partners.

Wait Time for Parent No-Show: Thirty minutes is usually considered a reasonable amount of time to wait for the other parent at an exchange location. This means that after thirty minutes, you return back home. The allowable window of time is really up to you and the other parent. You might want to consider adding some extra time if the other parent contacts you to say she'll be late, but if this becomes a pattern that feels manipulative,

> "When my ex tries to get all sly and change things up, I tell him the page of the parenting plan and what it says. He always says then that he's going to take me to court, but he never has."
>
> —Hattie, 32

you don't need to agree to it. Of course, you'll want to document this failure to pick up. And remember to try to stay neutral and not get the children involved in your conflict with your ex. Hard, I know, but you've got to keep trying for the sake of your kids.

Right of First Refusal and Who Can Watch Your Child: There is something in custody arrangements called "right of first refusal," which means that if you or the other parent can't have the child on a scheduled night, you need to give the other parent the opportunity to have the child at his home. You can also stipulate that "right of first refusal" doesn't apply if, say, the other parent is going to be gone for thirty minutes or less on a night he has your child. If someone does need to watch your child, the parenting plan should spell out who is allowed to watch the child. Perhaps a babysitter or older sibling would be all right with you, but not someone known to you to also be a gaslighter, such as an in-law or new spouse. These are the kinds of things to work out in your plan.

Keeping Divorce Documents and Parenting Plan Away from Children: Gaslighters will often leave sensitive divorce papers or parenting plans in plain sight to show their children how "unreasonable" their ex is. Or they'll want the kids to see that they give the ex "plenty of money." When confronted, the gaslighter may lie and say it wasn't his fault that your child was snooping. Make it a point in the parenting plan that any documentation related to your divorce or parenting plan is kept out of view of your children, and that it never be discussed with your children.

Only Respectful Talk When the Children Are in Each Parent's Custody: Sometimes exes think kids aren't paying attention while they talk disparagingly to someone else about the kids' other parent. Gaslighters may act as though they didn't know your kids were within earshot when complaining about you. They'll claim, "I didn't know the children were listening" or "It's not my fault they overheard a private conversation." If you spell out in your parenting agreement that the other parent can only be spoken about respectfully, gaslighters can't get away with this or they will be in violation of the agreement. (And take care not to be guilty of this behavior yourself.)

Method of Communication: If you have had issues with a gaslighter making volatile phone calls, or denying things he said when on the phone, it can be added to the parenting plan that communication will be done only through texting and e-mailing. Just using written communication gives you proof of what is said between you and your ex. You can also agree in the parenting plan that you will use schedule-sharing websites or apps. For more information on these types of services, see the Resources section at the end of this book.

Parent Coordinators

Finally, a word about other resources available to you. Parent coordinators are usually mental health professionals or other helping professionals. They are either appointed by a judge in family court, or you can hire one on your own. Some states even have certified parent coordinators, who have received extra training in how to help parents in high-conflict divorces. Parent coordinators will work with you and the other parent to make sure everyone agrees on using respectful communication, keeping children out of disagreements, and following the agreed-upon parenting plan. If there is a disagreement between you and the other parent, the parent coordinator can hear both sides of the discussion and give a recommendation, based on what is in your parenting plan and what is in the best interests of your child.

"I have a restraining order against my ex. We talk through a parent coordinator that the judge gave us. It has made my life so much less stressful."

—*Jana, 28*

HELP IS AVAILABLE!

As you know, gaslighters can cause a lot of psychological damage to you and your children. If left unchecked, gaslighting parents can do years of damage to a child. That's why I recommend counseling. There is absolutely nothing to be ashamed of in asking for this kind of help. Having a neutral third party to talk with will reduce the likelihood of stress-related illnesses, help heal grief, and reduce the chances of you and your children using unhealthy coping mechanisms.

Get Counseling for Your Children

When children have a gaslighting parent, it is very important that they receive help from a mental health professional, be it a social worker, a counselor, a psychologist, or someone else with training in dealing with the emotional lives of kids. Your children, regardless of their age, are most likely a victim of the gaslighter. In fact, children are often direct targets of gaslighters' abuse. This is because children are particularly vulnerable—they love their parents regardless of how those parents treat them. The gaslighter knows this and uses it to manipulate and also alienate your children from you.

In counseling, your children can discover that healthy parents do not act this way, and can learn how to cope with a parent who is a manipulator. The mental health professional can also meet with you and your child together in sessions. This can result in a better understanding of how your child feels and how you can best help him. Some mental health professionals are trained in play therapy. This is a way for your children to express their feelings when words don't come as easily to them. For more information on play therapists, see the Resources section at the end of this book.

Get Counseling with the Gaslighting Parent

Another option for counseling is for you and the gaslighting parent to attend therapy sessions together. Your mental health professional may even recommend having a therapy session for the whole family. Be aware that very cunning gaslighters have been able to fool even seasoned therapists, and sometimes family counseling with exes can lead to more damage. Consider your counselor's recommendation and your intuition when making this decision. The success of this type of therapy depends on the quality of the therapist and her knowledge of child development and gaslighting or narcissistic and antisocial behavior.

Get Counseling on Your Own

If you've been married to and now divorced from a gaslighter, getting counseling for yourself is imperative. You have gone through stresses that other parents don't typically face. This can lead to you feeling isolated, especially when your friends don't "get it." Your friends may not fully understand just how crazy-making your ex is, and you may not talk about it as much with them. A mental health professional can help you learn good self-care and more effective parenting strategies. Counseling is a safe place to get out your frustration and anger toward your gaslighting ex.

If you don't talk it out, you tend to act it out. This means that you may be drawn to unhealthy coping mechanisms, such as drinking or overeating. Also, unfortunately, holding in all that frustration can come out as impatience, frustration, and anger toward your children. Even though you would never choose to let your frustration out on your children, it can sneak through in various ways if you are under extreme stress. Counseling is highly recommended if you:

- Are snapping at your children or others
- Find yourself being more "rigid" concerning expectations of your children
- Find yourself getting angrier with your children
- Punish your children for minor issues
- Are tougher or unkind toward a child that looks more like the gaslighting parent than do your other children
- Are falling short on fulfilling your parental duties toward the children

Chapter 12 offers more details on counseling.

Practice Good Self-Care

In an airplane emergency, they tell you to put on your own oxygen mask before your child's so you can be an effective support. Likewise, you need to practice good self-care so you can be the best parent you can be. Co-parenting with a gaslighter can leave you feeling worn out, used, angry, and disappointed. It is important to practice *proactive* self-care, where you are taking good care of yourself on a regular basis, rather than *reactive* self-care, where you only take care of yourself when a crisis happens.

You may feel the need to make up for the gaslighting parent's behavior. However, this is impossible to do. You may also feel guilt for "sticking" your child with a pathological parent. Sometimes parents try to be a "perfect parent" to make up for what the other parent is lacking. This results in you getting burned out and actually makes you less effective as a parent. It is impossible to be a perfect parent, but there are a million ways to be a great parent. What do kids want most from their parents? Love, healthy boundaries, a good listener, and someone who understands them.

Your job is just to be the best parent you can be, regardless of the other parent's behavior. A trap the nongaslighting parent falls into is working to exhaustion to provide everything that the gaslighting parent doesn't give the child. You have the right to do less than what is humanly possible.

Divorcing and then coparenting with a gaslighter is one of the toughest things you will do. It is important to know your rights and your children's rights. Take good care of yourself, as it's a challenge to be the best parent you can be when you aren't on your game. This includes seeking counseling—it gives you a healthy outlet for your frustration, and a counselor can help you come up with solutions to make you and your child's lives better. There is hope, and your child can grow up to be a happy, healthy adult.

———

FROM DOING SOME soul-searching in this process, you may have realized that you are doing some gaslighting behaviors. It's common to pick up behaviors if you lived with a gaslighter. It may have been your way to cope with a situation out of control—by using the gaslighter's own manipulation strategies against him. In the next chapter, you'll learn how to stop these gaslighting tendencies in their tracks—making a better life for you and your loved ones.

11

WHO, ME?

What to Do When You Are the Gaslighter

WE'VE TALKED ABOUT GASLIGHTING IN MANY DIFFERENT RELATION-
ships and scenarios throughout this book. Now, it's time to
address an elephant in the room: What if you suspect that *you* are a gaslighter? The good news is that people who think they are gaslighters generally aren't. Throughout the book, I'm sure you've observed that true
gaslighters think they are totally fine and everyone else has a problem;
they have what is called an ego-syntonic personality. True gaslighters
would be the last people to seek psychological help. Which is not to say
that you might not have some gaslighting traits. If you see yourself as
someone with gaslighting behaviors, and you are willing to learn about
getting better, you are on the right track here. One of the biggest steps
toward making lasting change in your life is acknowledging that you
need help.

In this chapter, you will be able to pinpoint which gaslighting behaviors you may practice and start working on those. You may iden-

tify some of these behaviors in yourself right away, and others may come as a surprise. You will learn why you gaslight (usually because someone close to you is or was a gaslighter and taught you to be one as well). I want you to understand that while you will have learned much from reading this book, there is also plenty of help available for you.

Many people with gaslighting behaviors go through life having difficulties maintaining good friendships, being in unhealthy (and possibly even abusive) relationships, and not feeling very good about themselves. They may wonder what they are doing wrong, and why life seems to be easier for others. Is any of this true for you? All these experiences are very common for those with gaslighting behaviors.

DO YOU HAVE GASLIGHTING BEHAVIORS?

If you are concerned you might be a gaslighter, look at this list and see if you recognize any of these behaviors in yourself. You:

- Lie often, even in cases where lying doesn't serve a purpose
- Aren't direct in telling someone your needs
- Expect people to read your mind and know what you want
- Aren't sure what constitutes your needs
- Get upset when others can't figure out your needs
- Try to get people to do what you want instead of just directly asking them
- Don't tell people what you want, and then get back at those people. This is known as passive-aggressive behavior, which you will learn about later in this chapter.
- Are frustrated when others take more time doing something than you would like
- Have friends and family that tell you that your tone of voice is sarcastic or rough
- Have a short temper

- "Black out" and don't remember things that you did when you were angry
- See people as mainly selfish and out for their own needs

Well, what do you think? Are you ready for a deeper dive?

FLEAS

In Chapter 8 on gaslighting parents, we talked about the term *fleas*, as in, "If you lie down with dogs, you'll get fleas." People often learn to gaslight from their parents. We look to our parents for cues about how to act as adults—so it is normal to pick up some of their behaviors. If you now show some gaslighting behaviors, chances are you learned them as a form of self-preservation and coping in an abusive or chaotic home. The difference between someone with some gaslighting behaviors and a full-on gaslighter is that true gaslighters use these manipulative behaviors *as their only method of relating to the world*. That is, true gaslighters use these behaviors in all facets of their lives: home, work, social life, and in the community. My hunch is that you exhibit some of these behaviors when you are under stress or when you are dealing with a true gaslighter, most likely your parent. Please don't worry. You'll learn much from this chapter that can help you put your own behavior into context and help steer you toward healthier ways of relating and responding under stress.

SELF-PRESERVATION

When I say that your gaslighting behaviors were likely a form of self-preservation, I mean they were the way you protected yourself from harm. You did what you needed to do to cope and survive. If you lived with a gaslighting parent, you learned coping strategies so as to not be on the receiving end of your parent's wrath. You learned to lie about even inconsequential things, because your parent was so easily angered. You may be carrying the same self-preservation skills into adulthood.

WHAT IS A HEALTHY RELATIONSHIP?

If you witnessed unhealthy relationships while growing up, or have been in an unhealthy relationship, it may be difficult to know what makes up a truly healthy relationship. Let's take a look at the components of a healthy relationship. They include:

- Speaking freely about you and your loved one's needs and wants
- Listening openly to each other's concerns, without unnecessary interruption
- Refraining from bringing up past issues when they are unrelated to the topic being discussed
- Having boundaries, or limits, for what behavior is acceptable and what is not
- Socializing separately with friends without triggering jealousy or irrational behavior
- Pursuing separate interests without inducing insecurities
- Addressing concerns as they happen, rather than "stonewalling"
- Realizing that people are imperfect
- Receiving a loved one's "no" respectfully.

Note that when we grow up with gaslighting parents, or have been in gaslighting relationships, we tend to think that the complete absence of arguing is a sign of health. Even people in healthy relationships argue—in fact, arguing can be a healthy way of letting your needs be known to your partner. It's *fighting* that is the issue. It is healthy for couples to disagree as long as they address those issues in a respectful manner.

Open Communication

Having open, honest communication is an essential part of a healthy relationship. Keep in mind that honest and open communication is not the same as being "brutally honest" or cruel. You can speak your truth without it being harsh or damaging to the other person.

"I feel" Statements

One of the ways to get your needs across is to use "I feel" statements. In "I feel" statements, you are saying your concern in a respectful way, without blaming the other person. Let's say there are dirty dishes in the sink when you get home from work. An unhelpful thing to say to your child would be: "I work all day to pay for things—the least you can do is put the dishes in the dishwasher." This usually results in the dishes' still not going in the dishwasher. You did not get the intended result and you now have an argument going with your child.

With "I feel" statements, you state your concern without using the word *you*. People automatically get defensive when they feel accused, and when *you* is attached to a criticism, they tend not to hear the rest of what you are saying. Also, not using *you* helps you become part of the solution. In "I feel" statements, you say how you feel about an issue, why the issue is a concern to you, and you add a possible solution. As an alternative to the dishwasher statement above, an "I feel" statement would be: "When I come home to dishes in the sink, I feel frustrated because I like coming home to a clean home. I'd like the dishes to be put in the dishwasher right after eating."

Note that you are saying *exactly* what you want your child to do, whereas in the first example you were not. In the first example, you said what bothered you without giving any clear directions to your child. People like knowing exactly what is expected from them, and "I feel" statements do so in a constructive way.

The structure of an "I feel" statement is "When _____
_____ happens, I feel _____
because _____. A solution is
_____."

It may feel really odd to speak in "I feel" statements at first, especially when you have used another style of communication for years. But just try it once and see how it works. When you see how effective it is, you'll probably find yourself using "I feel" statements more and more.

Developing a Healthy Communication Style

In your quest to be healthier, it's helpful to look at how you interact and communicate with others. There are three main styles of communication: passive, aggressive, and assertive. Let's look at each one and which is best for healthy communication.

Passive Communication: An example of a passive statement might be: "Sure, you can borrow my sweater," when your grandma gave you that sweater and really you don't want anyone touching it. Passive statements are usually said in a quieter voice and without much eye contact. In passive communication, what's being conveyed is "I'm not okay, you're okay." You don't state your own needs, you placate, trying to make the other person happy, while ignoring what you want. Very often, people learn to do this with a gaslighting parent so he doesn't get out of control.

Aggressive Communication: In aggressive communication, on the other hand, the setup is "I'm okay, you're not okay." You state your needs without considering the other person. An example of an aggressive statement is: "Hell no, you're not borrowing my sweater. You'd look ugly in it anyway." Your voice is louder than usual. Aggressive communication can also take the form of smiling while saying something vicious—a skill at which gaslighters are experts.

Passive-Aggressive Communication: And then there's the passive-aggressive speaking style, where you don't let your needs be known, but you act out toward the other person. You might say, "Sure, you can borrow my sweater," but you then "forget" to give the other person her mail, or talk badly about her. You are denying your rights *and* trampling on the other person.

Assertive Communication: In assertive communication, or "I'm okay, you're okay," you state your needs while also being respectful of the other person. "I'm sorry, I don't loan out that sweater." You are stating your needs (not giving out your sweater) in a respectful way. You are not calling the person names or using an angry tone. Assertive communication is the healthiest way to express your needs.

Let's say you have been asked to be the head of a committee at work, and you know you don't have the time to do it. A passive way to respond would be to agree, even though you really don't want to do it. An aggressive way of responding would be, "No, and never ask me again!" You've pretty much assured that people will be scared about asking you anything from then on. A passive-aggressive way to respond would be to say yes, you'll be on the committee—then, because it is taking up your time, you show up a half-hour late to meetings and don't answer committee e-mails.

An assertive response would be, "I won't be able to do that." Your answer gets to the point. It's respectful toward the other person, and even more important, it's respectful toward yourself.

Nonverbal Communication and Voice Tone

Pay attention to your body language when you are talking. You want to communicate that you are open. Arms folded across your chest gives the message "I'm not interested in what you are saying" or "I'm fed up." An open posture—no crossed arms or legs—conveys an attitude of give and take.

Gaslighters are very good at being *incongruent*—they'll say one thing and their facial expression communicates something else altogether. Healthy people are *congruent*—their facial expressions match what they are saying. When you are speaking with someone, be observant of whether your body language and facial expressions match.

Be aware not only of what you say, but how you say it. Voice tone accounts for quite a bit of your message. This is why using texting as a primary communication method causes a lot of strife between people. When you are not getting (or giving) the full tone of the message, what is said can so easily be misconstrued.

Your voice volume will tend to increase when you are upset about something. Be aware if your voice volume is ramping up, and make a concerted effort to keep your voice at regular speaking volume and at a nice, medium pitch.

Stay On an Equal Level When Communicating

Sometimes when you have gaslighting behaviors, you may "talk down" to people without realizing it. If you have been raised by a gaslighter, you may find that he talks down to you. The goal in a healthy relationship is to communicate as equals—where no one person is superior to the other. There is a "Parent Adult Child Model" (PAC) that is part of a counseling practice called Transactional Analysis developed by Eric Berne, MD. It shows how people communicate with one another, and how to improve communication so that partners and family members speak respectfully to one another.

We take on the role of a parent, child, or adult when we are talking with someone. When you speak to someone as a parent, you use such phrases as "you should," "you need to," "you ought to," "never," and "always." This implies criticism or giving permission to the other person, exactly what a parent might do. People who are speaking as a parent may exhibit aggressive nonverbal communication, such as pointing fingers, clenching fists, or standing too close. When you are speaking to someone as a child, on the other hand, you use more emotions than words. Instead of communicating, you cry or get angry. You may also say such phrases as "I want," "I need," or "I don't care." People speaking in the child role may also tease the person they are addressing, giggle, or sound whiny. They tend to squirm or act as though they can't hear the other person.

The goal in a healthy relationship is to have both parties speak as adults to each other. Communicating as adults means truly listening to each other and not passing judgment. It means not being defensive, and having a non-verbal open posture as you are talking. People speaking as adults seek to understand what the other person is saying. They will ask others questions about their views, and then offer their own ideas or suggestions—instead of forcing their opinion on others. When adults are communicating, they see more gray areas of human behavior. This means that people are complex in their needs and wants, and they aren't just "good" or "bad"—they have a wide range of feelings and behaviors. People speaking as adults can also calmly "agree to disagree," and not bring up past hurts.

The next time you are speaking with someone, look at whether you are in the role of a parent, child, or adult. As I mentioned before, if you have gaslighting behaviors, you may more typically take on the role of a parent. If you are dealing with a gaslighter, you may slip into more of a child role. Really examine the words and body language you use, and try to shape them into more of an adult role when communicating. For more information on the Parent Adult Child Model, see the Resources section at the end of this book.

MAYBE THE OTHER PERSON IS THE GASLIGHTER

One technique gaslighters use is called *projection*—they accuse someone else of being manipulative, when it is really the gaslighter doing the controlling and manipulating. Maybe this is what's happening with you. Has someone in your life accused you of being manipulative or a gaslighter? Did it feel silly, unbelievable, or "off" at first? Trust your gut on this. As you've seen, gaslighters are master manipulators and it can be hard to see reality for what it is. What often happens is that we call people on their gaslighting behavior, and they turn around and say it's you who is the actual gaslighter. They do this to distract you from continuing the conversation about their offending behavior. Gaslighters hate being called out on their behavior—it means that you are on to them.

Of course it's always possible that both people in a relationship have gaslighting behaviors. The relationship could have started with one gaslighter, and the other person developed gaslighting behaviors as a way to cope and speak the gaslighter's "language." Sometimes a non-gaslighter will try to beat gaslighters at their own game by employing the same distraction and manipulation techniques. However, no matter how much you try to gaslight someone back, it will not work. Gaslighters will always outdo you in manipulation and insults. Plus, there's an emotional price to pay for saying things that are not congruent with your personality and your values. Again, trust your gut. If you are accused of gaslighting, look very closely at the dynamics at play and see whether you're really at fault. Chances are, if your conscience is at all involved, you are not the one with the problem!

RIGHTING WRONGS

If you discover that you have, in fact, gaslighted someone, part of the healing process is to apologize to the friend or family member you have hurt. Taking responsibility for your behavior and working toward getting better are essential to not only your well-being, but your loved one's as well.

Apologize

Apologize for the damage and hurt you have caused the other person. Keep in mind that "I'm sorry *you* got upset about *my* yelling" is not a valid apology—you are putting the responsibility on the other person. An example of a proper apology is: "I'm sorry I have yelled at you. It was hurtful, and not conducive to having a healthy relationship. I am going to counseling to learn a better way of communicating, because the way I did it was wrong."

> "I told my brother I was sorry for being so manipulative. I wasn't expecting this, but he also apologized to me for some things he had done. It was a real turning point for us."
>
> —*Megan, 50*

You are naming the behavior, taking responsibility for it, acknowledging that it has caused the other person pain, and stating what you are doing at making it better.

Give Your Partner Space

As you will read later in this chapter, apologizing to your loved one and getting help is not a guarantee that this person will want to continue a relationship with you, or even want to continue communicating with you. Some damage can take a very long time to process. After apologizing, consider asking your loved one for what he might need from you right now. Don't be surprised if the answer is, "I need some time alone." Acknowledge that you respect and honor this request. Do not badger or disagree with what your loved one is requesting of you. Wait for him to contact you first.

If your loved one tells you he needs some time to think, spend this time healing and focusing on self-improvement. Counseling is one of the ways you can learn why you practiced gaslighting behaviors, how to stop using them, and how to behave in a healthier way. You can learn more about counseling in the next chapter.

> "I told my wife I was sorry, and she told me she needed some time to think. I panicked, and told her not to go. It just made things worse."
>
> —Jonathan, 38

What If These Steps Don't Work?

Many times when one person starts changing their behavior for the better, the relationship doesn't work out. You find that you are on different paths in life, or that the other person has been gaslighting you all along and you've been shouldering the blame. If your relationship ends, you will go through a grief process not dissimilar from recovering from a death. If you have gaslighting tendencies, having a relationship end can even bring up feelings of abandonment. I happen to think Elisabeth Kübler-Ross (2014) had it right when she delineated that grief has five stages. She said that you may not go through all these stages, you may skip around them, and you may not go through some of them at all. Her stages are more a guideline to let you know that what you are feeling after a loss is normal.

Stages of Grief

Denial and Shock: "This isn't really over. It can't be." You may feel like things "aren't real," or that you are in a dream or nightmare.

Anger: "She has no right to leave. She's probably having the time of her life." You feel irrationally angry and get frustrated with people who have nothing to do with your loss. You also feel anger toward yourself.

Bargaining: "I swear, if she comes back, I'll never yell again." You try to cut deals with your higher power or with yourself. "If X happens, I will do Y." However, X doesn't happen. So, you move on to another bargain. That one doesn't work, either.

Depression: "It may really be over. I have never felt this bad . . . . ever." You feel teary most of the time. Your limbs (arms and legs) feel heavy. You feel lethargic. You may even have suicidal thoughts, such as "I wish I could disappear" or "If I died all this pain would stop." If you are feeling suicidal, please stop reading now and contact the National Suicide Prevention Lifeline at 1-800-273-TALK (8255) or www.suicidepreventionlifeline.org. They are available 24 hours a day, 7 days a week. See also the Resources section at the back of the book for how to get immediate help.

Acceptance: "I've learned from this. I'm going to make sure my next relationship is healthier." You get to the point where you don't like the thing that happened, but you acknowledge it happened. You may even see some positives that came out of your loss. For example, you learned more about yourself; you started going to counseling; you met some good friends that were going through the same thing. You also may start practicing forgiveness. Forgiveness doesn't mean that what happened to you in the past is okay; it means you give up hope of the past being any different. You let it go and stop its power over you.

Letting Go

Whether you have a religious affiliation or not, the "Serenity Prayer" by Reinhold Niebuhr is a helpful guide for getting through a time of loss or crisis in your life. "God grant me the serenity to accept the things I cannot change; courage to change the things I can; and wisdom to know the difference."

The "wisdom to know the difference" can be one of the hardest parts about getting through a difficult time, such as a breakup—especially when you feel that you are to blame. Sometimes it just takes time and patience to heal from a loss. For more information on grief and loss, see the Resources section at the end of this book.

Remember that these feelings are temporary. As much as it hurts now, you will feel better. Loss is like getting hit by a huge wave. You feel as if you are floundering and you will never surface. But over time, the waves will get smaller and smaller, and eventually you'll just have a couple of waves of grief that hit you every so often. If you are ever at the point where you feel like you might hurt yourself or someone else, contact the National Suicide Prevention Lifeline. For more information on suicide prevention, see the Resources section at the end of this book.

Closure Is Overrated

If you feel you haven't been able to get through a breakup because you never got "closure," I'll let you in on a little secret: *closure is overrated*. You may never really get the closure you want. By *closure*, I mean hearing from your ex and having a sit-down or phone call "good-bye" talk, kind of like a "relationship postmortem." If you have been waiting to find out from your ex exactly what you did that caused her to leave you, you may be waiting a really long time. Meanwhile, life goes on. Besides, even if your ex told you why she left, the answer probably still would not fill the void you are experiencing. You would continue to question why, or whether she telling you the whole story. The best thing you can do is continue to work on yourself, so that you are emotionally at your best when the next opportunity for a relationship happens.

IN THE NEXT chapter, you will learn about counseling, a helpful way to heal yourself of gaslighting behaviors, and also heal from others who have gaslighted you. You will discover the counseling theories of client-centered therapy, cognitive-behavioral therapy, acceptance and commitment therapy, and solution-focused therapy. Each therapy brings something new and different to the mix, and sometimes people find that one type of therapy is more helpful to them than the others. Sometimes people find that a mix of techniques is most helpful. By learning more about the types of counseling, you can make decisions as to what type of counseling model might work best for you.

12

GETTING FREE

Counseling and Other Ways to Get Help

WHETHER YOU'VE BEEN A VICTIM OF GASLIGHTING OR YOU'VE noted tendencies in yourself, it can really help to consult with a mental health professional (MHP). Gaslighting can cause extreme stress (and if you've been coparenting with a gaslighter, it causes stress to your kids as well). Making sure that you take good care of yourself, in part by getting enough sleep, exercising, and practicing healthy eating habits, is a big part of self-care. Getting professional help is another part of the equation.

As noted in the previous chapter, if you were raised by gaslighters or in a relationship with one, you may have found you were even gaslighting yourself. You may have questioned your reality in other areas of your life, due to the gaslighter's brainwashing tactics. It takes a lot of strength to know that you need additional help, so you should be very proud of yourself. Asking for help is a strength, and not everyone is able to know they need help.

COUNSELING

If you have been a victim of gaslighting or if you have gaslighting tendencies, it can help you to seek talk therapy or counseling. Although counseling may just seem like sitting and chatting with someone, it is actually hard work. What you get out of it depends on how much effort you put into it. Expectations also make a difference. If you go into counseling with the attitude of "This might make some positive changes in my life," you will have better results than going in with the attitude of "I don't think this will work, but whatever." Go in with an attitude of willingness and curiosity and you're much more likely to get the insights and new coping and communication tools you're looking for.

You can find MHPs through referrals from family, friends, and others in your community. Your health plan provider may also be able to direct you to professionals whose services it will cover. You can also find MHPs via search engines and counseling websites and apps. See the Resources section at the end of this book for more information on finding an MHP.

Choosing the Right One

When you meet an MHP, you may "click" with that person or you may not. You may need to meet with a few MHPs to find one with whom you fit well. Listen to your intuition when deciding whether an MHP is a right fit for you. Your intuition is that gut feeling that tells you whether something is okay or not. If you grew up with gaslighting parents, your intuition may have told you that something was wrong with your parents' behavior. If you brought this up with your parents, they most likely told you that you were crazy and you had no idea what you were talking about. The same holds true if you are or were in a relationship with a gaslighter. It's important to acknowledge that your intuition is almost always correct and to connect with that feeling that tells you that something is good or not. It is almost always on target. As you are the one hiring the MHP, you have the right to opt out of working with anyone with whom you feel uncomfortable, however highly that person may have been recommended to you.

Some MHPs' style is to listen and provide feedback for you when asked. Others may be more direct with you, even interrupting you. (If you have gaslighting tendencies yourself, you may need someone more direct, since having gaslighting behaviors mean you can probably "steamroll" or manipulate people pretty well. You can even tell the MHP, "I need someone to be direct with me and call me out.")

> "I went to a couple of therapists before I found one that I felt I could really talk to."
>
> —Deon, 34

When you contact a counselor, ask her:

- Her license and credentials
- How much she charges
- If she is covered by your insurance (check with your insurance company, too, and get that information in writing—your insurance company is not obligated to honor oral statements)
- Her experience with gaslighting
- What therapeutic style she uses (note that most therapists use a combination of therapy styles):
  - Client-centered therapy
  - Cognitive-behavioral therapy
  - Dialectical behavior therapy
  - Acceptance and commitment therapy
  - Solution-focused therapy
- How long she expects counseling to last. The answer you are looking for is "It depends on the person," since every person's issues and needs are unique. No one should promise you a quick fix.

Many MHPs are now doing private pay only—they do not file insurance, and you pay them in full at the end of the session. You can ask MHPs whether they work on a sliding scale, meaning they allow you to pay according to what you can afford, within reason. Many community mental health centers provide sliding scale treatment.

If the MHP doesn't file insurance, ask for a receipt so you can file for reimbursement with your insurance company. Then, when you contact your insurance company about reimbursement for a counseling visit, ask how much it reimburses for a "nonparticipating provider"; that is, an MHP that doesn't take insurance. Usually your reimbursement percentage, or money paid back to you, is lower if the MHP is out of your insurance network.

A word of caution: Anytime you file a medical claim with your insurance company, whether it is for counseling or a broken leg, that information goes into a national clearinghouse called the Medical Information Bureau (www.mib.com). This information can be used to deny you life and disability insurance—and until the Affordable Care Act, was used to deny health insurance coverage. Due to this fact, and for keeping privacy, many people choose not to file with their insurance for counseling visits.

You can get your entire file from the Medical Information Bureau at www.mib.com. It lists your date of service, doctor name, and diagnosis. I recommend you get this file, because as was my experience, my doctor's office was off by one digit on a diagnostic code, and the incorrect diagnosis it gave me it would have impacted my chances of getting insurance. If you get your file and find that the information is incorrect, contact your doctor's office, and it will correct the error. Ask for proof of the error correction.

Also be aware that if you are going to be applying with your state bar to become an attorney, you may be asked about any mental health treatment you receive. If you are planning on going into the military, ask a Department of Defense recruiter for its latest policies on people who have had counseling or are taking psychiatric medications. (You'll learn more about psychiatric medications later in this chapter.)

Should You Talk to Others About Your Therapy?

It is a personal decision whether to disclose to others that you are going for counseling. You may find that your family and friends think it's really odd. Some family members may worry that "secrets" in the family will come out. Going to counseling is a courageous and good thing—you are acknowledging that you need some guidance with some things in your life. Everyone has issues, and you are strong enough to do something about those issues. Don't let the reactions of others deter you—or simply don't tell anyone and just go.

"In my family, you don't go to a counselor unless you are super crazy. It felt really weird going to see someone and talk about things I wouldn't even tell my close friends. But talking about stuff that I was ashamed to talk about . . . . it's freeing."

—*Alfonso, 37*

In the list on page 219, I mentioned a few different types of therapy. (There are many more, too, but these are the main ones in use now.) You may find that you "click" better with one type than another. You may also discover that most MHPs use a blend of different counseling theories. MHPs should be able to tell you whether they have training in a particular type of counseling theory or theories.

Let's take a look at these theories and see whether you resonate more strongly with one or another.

Client-Centered Therapy

Client-centered therapy is a type of counseling that is nondirective. This means that you are in the "driver's seat" in the counseling session, and the MHP is neutral. This means that the counselor doesn't try to steer you in a particular direction or give you advice.

Unconditional Positive Regard

"Unconditional positive regard" is a big part of client-centered therapy. This means that the MHP accepts you for who you are, and supports you no matter what issues you bring into the session. If you have been gaslighted, you may already feel severely judged, so client-centered therapy is a safe place to talk about your issues without judgments being made.

Being Genuine

Having an MHP that is genuine with you is another important part of client-centered therapy. This means that the MHP will be "real" with you, and may tell you how he is feeling about something. For example, if you are sharing that your mother gaslighted you into believing that you didn't have worth, the MHP may share with you that he is feeling angry that you were treated that way. When an MHP is genuine, he role models for you how to be vulnerable. Being vulnerable means being open to sharing who you are, and your thoughts. Being the victim of a gaslighter means that you had to usually conceal who you were, keep it hidden deep down—because you knew if you were vulnerable the gaslighter would see that as a sign to attack you. Learning how to be vulnerable again is a big step toward getting away from your gaslighter's shadow on your life.

Self-Concept

Self-concept is what you believe about yourself. It consists of your ideas and values. The gaslighter in your life may have told you that your ideas and values were wrong, or may have blatantly disregarded them. Time with the gaslighter may have changed your self-concept to one that is different from reality. Your gaslighter's criticism may have led you to believe that you don't have worth or are always wrong. Client-centered counseling can help you get back to who you are, and rebuild an accurate self-concept—that you are a good, honest, and confident person.

Cognitive-Behavioral Therapy

Cognitive-behavioral therapy (CBT) is a type of counseling that focuses, in part, on the inner monologue, or voice, that plays through your mind all day long. In CBT, it's not an event that makes you feel a certain way, it's *what you think about the event* that impacts how you feel about it.

Think of this process as written out this way:

Action → Belief → Consequence.

Something happens to you. You have thoughts about this thing that happened to you. These thoughts then determine how you feel. Let's say you step in a mud puddle on the way to work (Action). You think to yourself, "I can't believe I was so stupid. Everyone at work is going to make fun of me" (Belief). You wind up having a bad day at work (Consequence). However, let's say you step in a mud puddle on the way to work (Action) and think to yourself, "Ah, accidents happen. I'll have something to laugh about with my coworkers" (Belief). You wind up having a pretty good day (Consequence). According to this theory, what you think about an event changes the outcome, so why not think of something that works in your favor?

Stopping Negative Self-Talk

We all have recordings that play in our mind during the day. Yours could be your voice, your parent's voice, a teacher's voice, or anyone else who might have been critical toward you. Most people are not aware of this "inner dialogue." If you take time to stop and really listen to your inner voice, you may find that it is not saying kind things. It can be defeatist, demeaning, and downright cruel sometimes. It's the voice that says, "You're not that smart, you'll never get this done," when you are given a new assignment at work. It's the voice that says, "You'll never be good enough."

One way to stop the negative self-talk (or "negative cognitions" in CBT-speak) is to become more aware that you are doing it. Just becoming cognizant of your inner voice will go a long way toward stopping it. When you catch your inner voice saying something negative, visualize a stop sign popping up—or say the word *stop*. This stops your negative thought in its tracks. Then come up with a positive replacement. For example, "I'm never going to get better" turns into "I can get better." "I never do anything right" turns into "I'm okay just the way I am." It can be a challenge to change your thought pattern. The good news is that once you start doing it, it gets easier and easier—until one day you'll discover that the negative thoughts are all but gone. Thinking positive thoughts becomes a self-fulfilling prophecy. If you think you're going to have a good day, you probably will have a good day. So, why not give yourself a fighting chance?

Cognitive Distortions

When you are a victim of gaslighting, or are engaging in gaslighting behaviors, you tend to have what are called *cognitive distortions*. These are ways of thinking that work against you. These thoughts are called distortions because they warp the way we see ourselves and the world around us. Cognitive distortions include overgeneralizing, catastrophizing, minimizing, mind-reading, and personalizing. You may use these patterns of thinking as a kind of protective shield around you. Let's take a look at how they work.

Overgeneralizing: You practice overgeneralizing when you think that the way one event went means all events will go the same way. An example would be: "My one friend can't go to the movies; I have no friends." The chances are that you do have more friends. Very rarely in life are things "all or nothing." Try to catch yourself overgeneralizing and ask yourself, "Is this really true?" If you gaslight, you may have such thoughts as, "If he leaves, I will never be happy again," or "I had one bad day, my days are always bad." It's viewing the world through the eyes of an angry pessimist.

Catastrophizing: This is best described by the saying "Making a mountain out of a molehill." An example would be: "My girlfriend said we should talk over dinner tonight. This is the end of our relationship! I just know it!" You're coming up with conclusions for which you have no proof. This kind of response can also be changed by noticing it. The saying, "No use crying over spilled milk" may not make sense if you have a gaslighting parent. You know that something like spilling milk turns your parent into a screaming monster who will lecture you on how expensive milk is, how worthless you are for spilling it, and how, if you keep it up, your family will have no money for milk, when in reality, accidents just happen. Healthy people just say, "Oops!" and help their children clean up.

Minimizing: This is a classic behavior of addicts. "I drink two six-packs a night; that doesn't mean I have a problem." It's the opposite of catastrophizing—it's making a molehill out of a mountain. Minimizing is a form of denial. It's the equivalent of, "Nothing to see here . . . . move along." Getting an evaluation by a MHP or getting counseling from one can help you determine whether you do in fact have an issue with making things less of a big deal than they really are, and whether there is a problem in particular that you tend to minimize, such as alcohol use or a gaslighter's abusive behavior.

Mind-reading: "I know she's thinking that I'm useless." Mind-reading happens when you attribute thoughts to other people. If you have gaslighting tendencies, you may automatically think people are saying negative beliefs because someone in your life was constantly feeding you negative information about yourself. You can never be sure what others are thinking. The chances of you being psychic are pretty low, so it's in your best interest to assume that a person is thinking something positive about you. Besides, as we say in the field, what other people think of you is none of your business.

Personalizing: "She didn't say hi back to me. What a jerk." Maybe your friend was busy and didn't hear you say hello. Maybe she was distracted with other things. Very rarely in life are things personal. Even if someone *is* mad at you, that's about that person, not you.

Just by becoming more aware of these cognitive distortions, they will start to show up less and less in your thinking. These distortions will then start being replaced with positive thoughts instead. It's in your best interest, both emotionally and physically, to stop these detrimental forms of thinking.

Dialectical Behavior Therapy

Dialectical Behavior Therapy (DBT) is a type of cognitive-behavioral therapy. It can be helpful for people who are victims of gaslighting, have gaslighting behaviors, or both.

DBT was originally used to treat borderline personality disorder (BPD). BPD is characterized, in part, by "all or nothing" thinking. People with BPD tend to swing between idealizing people and devaluing them. They will put people on a pedestal—the person with BPD feels that a particular person is perfect and can do no wrong—and then inevitably that person will fall off and be seen as terrible and bad. People with BPD are also prone to self-injurious behavior (including cutting, stabbing, burning, and rubbing the skin with erasers) and suicidal behavior. You may have noticed these behaviors in the gaslighter in your life, or you may have experienced them. Gaslighting and BPD can go hand in hand, just as it is frequently seen with narcissistic personality disorder (NPD), histronic personality disorder (HPD), and antisocial personality disorder (ASD, or sociopathy).

In DBT, the focus is on improving your tolerance of stress, keeping your emotions on an "even keel," and improving your relationships with others. In DBT it is believed that we can find a balance between acceptance and change. While you may not be responsible for all the things that lead you to using gaslighting behaviors, you are fully responsible for choosing a different, healthier way to live. In DBT, you and your MHP figure out which behaviors to reasonably accept and understand due to experiences you've had, and which you should work on and change for you to become a healthier person. This dance between acceptance and change is the "dialectical" part of DBT.

Some of the key concepts in DBT are as follows:

Distress Tolerance

Distressing events will happen in our lives; they're unavoidable. Some people seem to handle upsetting events fairly well, while others have more difficulties with coping. If you have gaslighting behaviors, you may have difficulty coping with the curveballs life throws at you. You may have said to yourself that this unpleasant thing that happened was someone else's fault; or this shouldn't happen to you, or it's unfair; or this is the worst thing that has ever happened to you. You may have heard these exact statements from your gaslighting parent—we copy what we hear as children. Part of gaslighting is feeling that you are entitled to always have things go your way—when in life, this just isn't possible. In DBT, the acronym ACCEPT is used as a way to cope with unwanted events.

A = Activities—Get moving and do simple tasks to distract yourself from an upsetting event.

C = Contribute—Help out others to stop your self-focused behavior. This also helps distract you and broadens your view of life.

C = Comparisons—Look at how your life is different from those who have a lot less than you do. Again, focusing outside yourself helps you deal with upsetting events. A gratitude journal, where you write down every-thing you are thankful for and what is going right, is a way for you to focus on all the good in your life, instead of focusing on the upsetting parts.

E = Emotions—Act the opposite of whatever emotion you are hav-ing. If you are feeling tired, get active. If you are feeling sad, watch a funny movie. This practice shows you that emotions are temporary, and you have the power to change them. You may have heard the phrase, "Act as if "—act calm until you feel calm.

P = Push Away—If you are feeling that you're useless, visualize your-self feeling competent and making change in the world. This is a way of "pushing away" the negative feelings you are having at the moment.

T = Thoughts—Engage in activities that are not emotion-filled. Fo-cus more on the logical part of your thinking. Watch a movie that doesn't have heavy emotional content. Basically, become more like Spock for the time being—he was all logic, no emotion.

Psychological First-Aid Kit

When you have lived a chaotic life, it can be hard to come up with what you can do to take care of yourself and make yourself feel better. With a gaslighting parent, you may not have received tender loving care. You may not know how to treat yourself with loving kindness. It's especially difficult to do when you are in the middle of a crisis. What are some things you can do right now to feel good? Make a list of things or activi-ties that make you feel relaxed and calm. Put this list in a place where you will see it often, such as on your bathroom mirror or refrigerator. Take a photo of your list with your smartphone—this way you will always have it with you when you need it.

Examples include:

- Going for a walk
- Spending time with your pet
- Taking a bath
- Meditating
- Creating some art
- Writing in a journal
- Doing yoga
- Practicing deep breathing
- Listening to a creative visualization recording
- Calling a supportive friend or family member
- Going outside
- Eating a snack
- Drinking some water

Be Aware When You Are Getting "Wound Up"

Part of taking good care of yourself is knowing when your stress level is starting to feel out of control. When you have been gaslighted, or you have gaslighting behaviors, you may have difficulty with regulating your emotions. People who have learned to regulate their emotions know when they are getting upset and how to calm themselves down. You also tend to stay more on an even keel emotionally and have less mood swings when you can regulate how you are feeling. What does your body feel like when you are getting upset? People experience:

- Clammy hands
- Knots in their stomach
- Feeling hot or flushed
- Rapid heartbeat
- Shallow or rapid breathing
- Feeling that things "aren't real"

When you start feeling these sensations, stop and take a deep breath. Deep breathing, also called diaphragmatic breathing, happens when you are breathing using your full lung capacity. This is achieved by engaging your diaphragm, a muscle at the base of your lungs. If you are doing diaphragmatic breathing correctly, your belly should be expanding when you inhale. Try inhaling for a count of 5, then exhaling for a count of 10. When you practice diaphragmatic breathing, you are kicking in the parasympathetic part of your autonomic nervous system. This causes you to have a feeling of relaxation and peace. Try it the next time you feel a rush of stress or anxiety.

Another technique for decreasing feelings of stress is to name three things you can see, three things you can feel, and three things you can hear. This practice acts as a distractor and keeps you in the here and now. When you are in the here and now, also known as "being present," you are more likely to keep your feelings well regulated.

Acceptance and Commitment Therapy

The third and final form of counseling we'll look at is called acceptance and commitment therapy (ACT). In ACT, you feel your feelings instead of pushing them aside or ignoring them. Avoiding "icky" or uncomfortable feelings is a natural part of being human. However, the more you avoid a feeling, the more it comes back—and sometimes it comes back with a vengeance. One of the theories of ACT is that you need to fully feel a feeling to be able to come out on the other side of it and let it go.

In ACT, you are encouraged to be present with your feelings. You'll use a three-part process of observing yourself, feeling your feelings, and then letting them go. You also discover your personal values and formulate steps to act on those values. Some of the main processes, or tenets, of ACT, are mindfulness, cognitive diffusion, values clarification, acceptance, and committed action.

Mindfulness: *Mindfulness* simply means the ability to stay in the present moment. One of the ideas behind mindfulness, or being present, is that when we focus too much in the past, we're likely to feel depressed;

when we focus too much on the future, we're likely to feel anxious. Focusing on the present brings us a feeling of calm. You will learn more about practicing mindfulness later in this chapter.

Cognitive Diffusion: This term describes a process whereby you decrease your emotional connection to your thoughts and make them have less of a negative impact on you. The idea is that a thought is just a thought, and it doesn't have much bearing on who you really are or how you go about your life. One way of decreasing your emotional connection with your thoughts is to acknowledge that you are having the thought, such as that you are not a good person. When you tag it as just a thought you are having, the thought loses some of its power over you. Another cognitive diffusion technique is to repeat a negative thought in a silly voice in your head. Yet another technique is to "externalize" the mind: "Oh, that's just my mind doing its worrying thing." This takes the thoughts outside the self, so you are less likely to hang on to them.

Values Clarification: In ACT, we look at our values as a choice. A value is what gives your life meaning; it gives you a sense of purpose. One technique for understanding your values is to write down what you would want people to say at your funeral. "He cared about his kids. He was a loyal friend. He had a passion for his career." Another way to determine values is to figure out what you would value if no one knew of the achievements you have made in your life.

Acceptance: This is just what it sounds like. You accept the thoughts and feelings you are having so as to be able to take action. One technique of acceptance, "unhooking," involves acknowledging that just because you have a thought doesn't mean you are going to act on it. Another technique is to ask yourself whether this pattern of thought has worked in your life. Has it helped you become the person you want to be? Or is it holding you back? A counselor may also ask you to write down, or journal, the difficult things you have gone through. Getting things out of your mind and on to paper helps you process them or work them through.

Committed Action: In this step of ACT, you make a plan to act on your values, a set of goals, both short-term and long-term. You feel uneasy or "not right" when you are veering away from these goals on your life path. Let's say you discovered that one of your values in your life is to have a good relationship with your spouse. What steps can you take to meet those goals? Be specific about your goals. A broad goal might be: "I want my spouse to be happy." An immediate goal is something you can do in the next day. For example, "I will get home before dinner tomorrow." A short-term goal is something you can accomplish within a week. In this case, a realistic short-term goal could be: "I will call and schedule our family photos." A medium-term goal is something you can do within the next few months. This could be: "I will clean up the garage and finish all house projects." A long-term goal is something you can accomplish within the next few years, such as: "We will be debt-free in three years."

Solution-Focused Therapy

Solution-focused therapy looks at solving problems. It is focused on the present and future, rather than on the past. Solution-focused therapy doesn't look as much at your experiences and how you got to where you are today. It looks at how you can create a better tomorrow.

The Magic Question

A solution-focused MHP might ask you, "How would things be if they were well?" or "You wake up tomorrow, and everything is how you'd like it to be. Who would be the first person to notice?" The MHP is looking at your goals—what you would like to accomplish in your life. The MHP then helps you create building blocks to get there. Chances are, you haven't been asked those kinds of questions before. Contemplating what your best life would look like can be freeing and healing all on its own.

Change One Thing

One of the premises of solution-focused therapy is that you don't need to change a whole bunch of behaviors to see positive changes in your life. You can change just one thing, and everything in your life can change. For example, you decide that you are going to start thanking your spouse when you see him doing chores around the house. You notice over time that you and your spouse seem to be getting along better—and you no longer have to ask for something to get done around the house. Just that one thing changed the dynamic of your relationship.

Give Yourself Credit

The fact that you are reading this book shows that you have taken the initiative to make change in your life. That is a pretty amazing thing, and a sign that you have a lot of strength. Gaslighters are good at psychologically beating down their victims—and as a result you may be very tough on yourself, and blaming yourself for things that aren't your fault. In solution-focused therapy, the MHP helps you see all the strides you have made—things you may not have noticed before. It's important that someone helps us see all the progress we've made, especially when we feel like we're "stuck." Progress is progress, it doesn't matter whether it was an inch forward—you still made the effort and succeeded.

What Is Going Well?

A solution-focused MHP may ask you what is going well in your life right now, or what has provided you relief from the gaslighting you've experienced. It may be that when you exercise it helps clear your mind and decreases your anxiety. You may find that when you are engrossed in a hobby that you temporarily forget about the suffering you endured, and don't hear the gaslighter's voice in your head. Your MHP will help you see when things are better in your life, so you can increase those activities or people in your life. What you focus on grows.

GROUP VERSUS INDIVIDUAL THERAPY

Group therapy can be more cost-effective than individual therapy. You may be more likely to attend therapy and get more out of it if it's in a group setting rather than individual. There is positive social pressure in a group—you are more likely to show up at the next session because you are expected to by the other group members. You can experience something called "universalization" in group therapy. This is the feeling that you are not the only one with these particular concerns or issues. Feeling that sense of belonging can be very healing and cathartic. You can do group therapy at the same time you are doing individual therapy—and this can increase the benefits (Echeburúa, Sarasua, and Zubizarreta 2014). You can even attend group and individual therapy via video conferencing.

MEDICATION

When you meet with an MHP, he may refer you to a prescriber for medication to help with anxiety or depression. Anxiety and depression are common when you have been dealing with a gaslighter. Sometimes your thought processes may become clouded due to your reality being questioned, or due to lack of sleep. It can be a challenge to absorb what you are learning in counseling if you are feeling really worn out. It may be difficult to even summon up enough energy to attend your counseling session. Antidepressant medication can help you feel less "clouded" and may help you sleep better. When you don't get enough sleep, it can really do a number on your brain and body. Just getting a good night's rest can reduce some anxiety and depression symptoms. Side effects of antidepressants include dry mouth and nausea.

MEDITATION

Meditation is another powerful tool for working with your gaslighting experiences, thoughts, and behaviors. It has been found to improve our positive feelings toward others and ourselves. Meditation is focusing on your breath. At its most basic, the goal of meditation is to spend some quiet time with your thoughts, not to empty your mind—even people who have been meditating for years find that difficult to do. The goal is just to notice yourself inhaling and exhaling.

Mindfulness Meditation

Mindfulness is a type of meditation that has become very popular. Mindfulness is used in both DBT and ACT. You read about its use in ACT earlier in this chapter. With other "focused" forms of meditation, you are usually sitting or lying down. With mindfulness practice, distractions are actually welcomed. When you have a distraction or a thought pop into your mind, just acknowledge it and let the thought pass. If it's important, it will go on your mind's back burner until you need to retrieve it.

Eating mindfully practice: You may be someone who eats more than you should when you're upset. You may be used to chomping off big pieces of food and swallowing them almost whole and without even really tasting them, because you tend to be distracted while eating. Being distracted can help us not have to deal with issues and feelings, but those issues are bound to come out in other ways—like overeating. Mindful eating can be especially helpful for you. When you eat mindfully, you just focus on your food—you don't watch TV, play on your phone, or read something. You chew each piece of food at least ten times and focus on all the sensations—smell, taste, texture, etc.

You can also try eating off a smaller plate. Your brain is easy to fool, and it thinks that when a small plate of food has been eaten, it was just as much food as on a large plate. If you are just focusing on your food, you may realize the food you're eating you don't even really like. Many people have started eating healthier proteins and fresh fruits and vegetables once they really started focusing on their food.

You can also practice mindful cooking. You may tend to skip going to the grocery store or cooking your own food because you forget or run out of time. Or you think you don't like to cook. When you spend time cooking your own food, you usually wind up appreciating it more, eating less, and still feeling satiated or full. You can even turn dishwashing into a mindfulness practice.

Walking mindfulness practice: In his book *Peace Is Every Step*, Thich Nhat Hanh (1992) describes a walking mindfulness practice. You walk at a slower pace than usual. When you put your foot down, focus on how your feet feel on the earth, and how the sun and breeze feel on your face. If you see something pleasant, like a tree, just stop and observe it. When you put your other foot down, refocus all over again. This is a great practice for someone with a particularly active and jumpy mind.

WHAT IF ALL THESE THINGS DON'T WORK?

Sometimes enough damage has been done by gaslighters and gaslighting behaviors that it can feel like you are stuck and things aren't going to get better. It's important to remember that getting better takes time. Your all-or-nothing thinking may be telling you that because a treatment didn't work right away that there are no more options. That is simply not true.

If you feel that you aren't making any progress, ask yourself the following questions:

- Have I fully committed to getting better? (Sometimes people hold on to old behaviors because they get *secondary gains* from them. You might be getting attention when you cause drama among your friends and family. You might be feeling a sense of power over being able to manipulate others.)
- Have I gone into the treatment with a positive attitude? (Studies have found that if you go into therapy with positive expectations, you are more likely to have a good outcome.)

Keep in mind that treatments aren't "one size fits all." A treatment that worked for a friend of yours may not necessarily work for you. It can be frustrating, but once you find a treatment that is a good fit for you, things move along at a pretty good pace.

YOU MADE IT TO THE END

So, you've made it through the gaslighting maze. Congratulations! Hopefully you have gained a lot of information on how to cope with people that make your life very difficult (even if that also includes yourself).

One of the best ways to extract yourself from gaslighting is to limit or stop contact with gaslighters. However, in some situations, such as coparenting, this is not an option. In cases where you can't get away from the gaslighter, it's important to maintain healthy boundaries, seek out support, and consult mental health and legal professionals for additional help. If you work with or for a gaslighter, remember that there are laws that can protect you if you are harassed.

Gaslighters can wield a lot of power—not just in your family, but also on a national and international level. You learned how gaslighters can quickly turn into dictators and cult leaders, making it virtually impossible to know what is truth and fabricated truth. Having citizens that think independently is the bane of gaslighting leaders, so keep as educated about current events and gaslighting as possible. Gaslighting can be perpetuated by the media—if a news story seems biased or off, it usually is. It is your right to speak out as a concerned citizen, and also make your voice heard through voting.

Hope is eternal—there is always something you can do to make your life circumstances better, regardless of the severity of gaslighting to which you are subjected. Making positive changes—such as getting away from the gaslighter, setting boundaries, and speaking out—may not be easy at first, but the benefits of greater peace of mind, happier children, and better health are worth it.

RESOURCES

Adult Children of Alcoholics
www.adultchildren.org

Attorneys and Mental Health Professionals
American Association for Marriage and Family Therapy (AAMFT)
www.aamft.org
American Bar Association
www.americanbar.com
American Mental Health Counselors Association
www.amhca.org
American Psychological Association
www.apa.org
National Association of Social Workers
www.socialworkers.org
Psychology Today Directory
www.psychologytoday.com/us/therapists

Caregiving

N. L. Mace. *The 36-Hour Day: A Family Guide to Caring for People Who Have Alzheimer Disease, Related Dementias, and Memory Loss.* Boston: Grand Central Life & Style, 2012.

National Alliance for Caregiving
www.caregiving.org

Contacting US Officials and Agencies

Elected Officials
https://www.usa.gov/elected-officials
Government Agencies
https://www.usa.gov/agencies

Coparenting

J. S. Gaies and J. B. Morris. *Mindful Co-parenting: A Child-Friendly Path Through Divorce.* CreateSpace Independent Publishing Platform, 2014.

Our Family Wizard
www.ourfamilywizard.com
AppClose
www.appclose.com
2Houses
www.2houses.com

Cults and Recovery from Cults

Cult Education Institute
www.culteducation.com
Cult Research
www.cultresearch.org
Freedom of Mind Resource Center
www.freedomofmind.com

Domestic Violence

DomesticShelters.org
www.domesticshelters.org
The National Domestic Violence Hotline
www.thehotline.org
1-800-799-7233

Employee and Employer Rights

Equal Employment Opportunity Commission (EEOC)
www.eeoc.gov
EEOC: File a Charge of Employee Discrimination
https://publicportal.eeoc.gov
EEOC: Title VII of the Civil Rights Act of 1964
https://www.eeoc.gov/laws/statutes/titlevii.cfm

Family Law Attorneys

Family Law Organization
www.familylaw.org

Help for Minors / Recovery from Childhood Abuse

Childhelp National Child Abuse Hotline (US and Canada)
1-800-422-4453
www.childhelp.org/hotline
Child Welfare Information Gateway
State Child Abuse and Neglect Reporting Numbers
https://www.childwelfare.gov/organizations
K. Roth and F. B. Friedman. *Surviving a Borderline Parent: How to Heal Your Childhood Wounds and Build Trust, Boundaries, and Self-Esteem*. Oakland, CA: New Harbinger Publications Inc., 2004.

How Congress Voted

www.ballotpedia.org
www.congress.gov/roll-call-votes
www.govtrack.us
www.opensecrets.org

Legal Services

www.findlegalhelp.org
www.probono.net
US Department of Justice
https://www.justice.gov/eoir/list-pro-bono-legal-service-providers

Parent Adult Child Model

Thomas Harris. *I'm OK—You're OK*. New York: Harper Perennial, 2004.

Personal Information Search Websites
www.instantcheckmate.com
www.peoplefinders.com
www.radaris.com
www.spokeo.com
www.zabasearch.com

Play Therapists
Association for Play Therapy
www.a4pt.org

Sexual Assault
National Sexual Assault Hotline
www.rainn.org
(800) 656-4673

STD Testing
Planned Parenthood
www.plannedparenthood.org
1-800-230-7526

Suicide Prevention
National Suicide Prevention Lifeline
https://suicidepreventionlifeline.org
1-800-273-8255

Workplace Firearms or Weapons Attack
www.gov.uk/government/publications/stay-safe-film

Workplace Harassment
Advisory, Conciliation and Arbitration Service (Acas)
0300 123 1100
18001 0300 123 1100 (for customers with a hearing/speech impairment)
Available Monday to Friday, 8am to 6pm
Acas Leaflet, "Bullying And Harassment at Work: A Guide for Employees"
http://www.acas.org.uk/media/pdf/r/1/Bullying-and-harassment-
at-work-a-guide-for-employees.pdf

ACKNOWLEDGMENTS

Thank you to my family, human and canine—R. Michael Sitz, William Moulton, Claude Moulton, Esq., Christine Whitney, Esq., Lucy Sarkis, Scamp Moulton, and Rocky Moulton. A very special thank you to editor Caroline Pincus, who made my writing make much more sense. Thank you to Renée Sedliar at Da Capo Press, who acquired the book and has been its champion, and to my agent, Carol Mann. Thank you to Ari Tuckman, PsyD, MBA, Roberto Olivardia, PhD, Jeremy S. Gaies, PsyD, Karl N. Klein, Esq., and Valerie Theng Mattherne, Esq., for consultation and support.

REFERENCES

"Alexander Litvenenko: Profile of Murdered Russian Spy." 2016. *BBC News*, January 21. Accessed February 20, 2018. http://www.bbc.com/news/uk -19647226.

American Psychiatric Association. 2013. *Diagnostic and Statistical Manual of Mental Disorders (DSM-5)*. American Psychiatric Publishing.

Batty, D. and Cherubini, E. 2018. "UK universities accused of failing to tackle sexual misconduct." *The Guardian*. March 28. Accessed August 10, 2018. https://www.theguardian.com/world/2018/mar/28/ uk-universities-accused-failing-tackle-sexual-misconduct.

Bernstein, D. 2017. "Blago: His Life in Prison." *Chicago*, September. http:// www.chicagomag.com/Chicago-Magazine/October-2017/Blago-His -Life-in-Prison/.

Boeckel, M. G., A. Wagner, and R. Grassi-Oliveira. 2017. "The Effects of Intimate Partner Violence Exposure on the Maternal Bond and PTSD Symptoms of Children." *Journal of Interpersonal Violence* 32 (7): 1127–1142.

Boyle, R. 2015. "Employing Trafficking Laws to Capture Elusive Leaders of Destructive Cults." *Oregon Review of International Law* 17 (2), St. John's Legal Studies Research Paper No. 15-0030. https://papers.ssrn.com/sol3/papers.cfm?abstract_id=2690453.

Byers, P. 2017. "Facebook estimating 126 million people were served content from Russia-linked pages." CNN Media, October 31.

Center for Responsive Politics. 2017. National Rifle Association. https://www.opensecrets.org/orgs/summary.php?id=d000000082.

Cialdini, R. 2009. *Influence: Science and Practice.* 5th ed. Boston: Allyn and Bacon.

Cloud, D. S. 2017. "Lawmakers Slam Social Media Giants for Failing to Block Russian Ads and Posts During 2016 Campaign." *Los Angeles Times*, November 1. http://www.latimes.com/nation/la-na-social-media-russia-20171101-story.html.

Donatone, B. "The Coraline Effect: The Misdiagnosis of Personality Disorders in College Students Who Grew Up with a Personality Disordered Parent." *Journal of College Student Psychotherapy* 30, no. 3 (2016): 187–196.

Ellison, S. 2017. "Everybody Knew: Inside the Fall of Today's Matt Lauer." *Vanity Fair*, November 29. Accessed January 21, 2018. https://www.vanityfair.com/news/2017/11/inside-the-fall-of-todays-matt-lauer.

Ellman, M. 2002. "Soviet Repression Statistics: Some comments" *Europe-Asia Studies* 54(7): 1151–1172.

Fisher, M. 2013. "Kim Jong Un Just Had His Own Uncle Killed. Why?" *Washington Post*. December 12. Accessed April 13, 2018. https://www.washingtonpost.com/news/worldviews/wp/2013/12/12/kim-jong-un-just-had-his-own-uncle-killed-why/?noredirect=on&utm_term=.a136e244dd9c.

Goffard, C. 2017. "Dirty John." Audio blog post, September 11–October 8. https://itunes.apple.com/us/podcast/dirty-john/id1272970334?mt=2.

Gregory, S., R. J. Blair, A. Simmons, V. Kumari, S. Hodgins, and N. Blackwood. 2015. "Punishment and Psychopathy: A Case-Control Functional MRI Investigation of Reinforcement Learning in Violent Antisocial Personality Disordered Men." *Lancet Psychiatry* 2 (2): 153–160.

Hahn, T. N. 1992. *Peace Is Every Step.* New York: Bantam.

Harris, K. J., E. Gringart, and D. Drake. 2017. "Leaving Ideological Groups Behind: A Model of Disengagement." *Behavioral Sciences of Terrorism and Political Aggression*, 1–19.

Hayes, C. 2017. "Venezuelan President Eats Empanada on Live TV While Addressing Starving Nation." *Newsweek*, November 3. Accessed February 20,

2018. http://www.newsweek.com/venezuelan-president-eats-empanada-live-tv-while-addressing-starving-nation-701050.

International Labour Organization. 2012. "New ILO Global Estimate of Forced Labour: 20.9 million victims." June 1. http://www.ilo.org/global/about-the-ilo/newsroom/news/WCMS_182109/lang-en/index.htm.

Isaac, M., and S. Shane. 2017. "Facebook to Deliver 3,000 Russia-Linked Ads to Congress on Monday." *New York Times*, October 1. https://nyti.ms/2yChMiJ.

Jaffe, P., M. Campbell, K. Reif, J. Fairbairn, and R. David. 2017. "Children Killed in the Context of Domestic Violence: International Perspectives from Death Review Committees." Pp. 317–343 in *Domestic Homicides and Death Reviews*. London: Palgrave Macmillan.

Jowett, G. S., and V. O'Donnell. 2018. *Propaganda & Persuasion*. 7th ed. New York: Sage Publications.

Kennedy, M. 2017. "NPR's Head of News Resigns Following Harassment Allegations." NPR, November 1. http://www.npr.org/sections/thetwo-way/2017/11/01/561363158/nprs-head-of-news-resigns-following-harassment-allegations.

Kessler, G. 2018. "Fact-checking President Trump's 'Fake News Awards.'" *Washington Post*, January 17. Accessed January 16, 2018. https://www.washingtonpost.com/news/fact-checker/wp/2018/01/17/fact-checking-president-trumps-fake-news-awards/?utm_term=.5481bbd6a6d5.

Knopp, K., S. Scott, L. Ritchie, G. K. Rhoades, H. J. Markman, and S. M. Stanley. 2017. "Once a Cheater, Always a Cheater? Serial Infidelity Across Subsequent Relationships." *Archives of Sexual Behavior* 46 (8): 2301–2311.

Kraus, A. 2016. "Parental Alienation: The Case for Parentification and Mental Health." PhD diss., Colorado State University.

Kübler-Ross, E., and D. Kessler. 2014. *On Grief and Grieving: Finding the Meaning of Grief Through the Five Stages of Loss*. New York: Simon and Schuster.

Kurtzleben, D. 2018. "Chart: How Have Your Members of Congress Voted on Gun Bills?" NPR. February 19, 2018. Accessed April 8, 2018. https://www.npr.org/2018/02/19/566731477/chart-how-have-your-members-of-congress-voted-on-gun-bills.

Lisi, B. 2017. "Venezuelan President Maduro Sneaks Bite of Empanada Tucked into Desk Drawer During State Broadcast." *New York Daily News*, November 2. http://www.nydailynews.com/news/world/president-maduro-sneaks-bite-empanada-state-broadcast-article-1.3607158.

Madrigal, A. C. 2018. "'Most' People on Facebook May Have Had Their Accounts Scraped." *Atlantic*, April 4, 2018. Accessed April 4, 2018. https://www.theatlantic.com/technology/archive/2018/04/most-people-on-facebook-may-have-had-their-accounts-scraped/557285/.

Matthews, C. H., and C. F. Salazar. 2014. "Second-Generation Adult Former Cult Group Members' Recovery Experiences: Implications for Counseling." *International Journal for the Advancement of Counselling* 36 (2): 188–203.

McDonald, S. E., E. A. Collins, A. Maternick, N. Nicotera, S. Graham-Bermann, F. R. Ascione, and J. H. Williams. 2017. "Intimate Partner Violence Survivors' Reports of Their Children's Exposure to Companion Animal Maltreatment: A Qualitative Study." *Journal of Interpersonal Violence*, 0886260516689775.

Merriam-Webster. 2018. "Propaganda." Accessed January 18, 2018. https://www.merriam-webster.com/dictionary/propaganda.

National Coalition Against Domestic Violence. 2017. Accessed December 27, 2017. http://www.ncadv.org.

National Sexual Violence Resource Center. 2012, 2013, 2015. "Statistics About Sexual Violence." Accessed February 26, 2018. https://www.nsvrc.org/sites/default/files/publications_nsvrc_factsheet_media-packet_statistics-about-sexual-violence_0.pdf

Oxford University Press. 2017. "Frenemy." Oxford English Dictionary Online. http://www.oed.com.

Patrick, W. 2017. "The Dangerous First Date." *Psychology Today*, December, 44–45.

Popken, B. 2017. "Russian Troll Tweets Duped Global Media and 40+ Celebrities." NBCNews.com, November 4. https://www.nbcnews.com/tech/social-media/trump-other-politicians-celebs-shared-boosted-russian-troll-tweets-n817036.

Radcliffe, J. "Rasputin and the Fragmentation of Imperial Russia." 2017. Young Historian's Conference, Portland State University. Accessed April 13, 2018. Available at https://pdxscholar.library.pdx.edu.

Radtke, M. 2017. "When War Is Bad Advice: Dictators, Ministerial Cronyism, and International Conflict." Accessed April 13, 2018. http://www.people.fas.harvard.edu/~jkertzer/HISC2017/schedule/papers/Radtke.pdf.

RGJ Archives. "Full Text of Marianne Theresa Johnson-Reddick's Obituary." 2013. *Reno Gazette-Journal*, September 10. Republished June 2014.

Romm, T. and K. Wagner. 2017. "Facebook Says 126 Million People in the U.S. May Have Seen Posts Produced by Russian-Government-Backed Agents." Recode, October 30. https://www.recode.net/2017/10/30/16571598 /read-full-testimony-facebook-twitter-google-congress-russia-election -fake-news.

Ryall, J. 2017. "Did Kim Jong-un Kill His Uncle and Brother Over 'Coup Plot Involving China'?" *Telegraph*. August 24. Accessed April 13, 2018. https://www.telegraph.co.uk/news/2017/08/24/did-kim-jong-un -kill-uncle-brother-coup-plot-involving-china/.

Sarkis, S. 2017. "11 Warning Signs of Gaslighting." *Here, There, and Everywhere* (blog). PsychologyToday.com, September 28. Accessed February 28, 2018. https://www.psychologytoday.com/blog/here-there-and -everywhere/201701/11-warning-signs-gaslighting.

Savage, M. 2018. "A third of women say they have faced sexual harassment at work." *The Guardian*. June 10. Accessed August 10, 2018. https:// www.theguardian.com/uk-news/2018/jun/10/third-of-women -say-they-have-faced-sexual-harassment-at-work.

Setoodeh, R., and E. Wagmeister 2017. "Matt Lauer Accused of Sexual Harassment by Multiple Women." *Variety*. November 29. Accessed January 21, 2018. http://variety.com/2017/biz/news/matt-lauer-accused-sexual -harassment-multiple-women-1202625959/.

Slavtcheva-Petkova, V. 2017. "Fighting Putin and the Kremlin's Grip in Neo-authoritarian Russia: The Experience of Liberal Journalists." *Journalism*, 1464884917708061.

Swanson, J. W., N. A. Sampson, M. V. Petukhova, A. M. Zaslavsky, P. S. Appelbaum, M. S. Swartz, and R. C. Kessler. 2015. "Guns, Impulsive Angry Behavior, and Mental Disorders: Results from the National Comorbidity Survey Replication (NCS-R)." *Behavioral Sciences & the Law* 33, no. 2–3: 199–212.

Treisman, D. 2017. *Democracy by Mistake*. (No. w23944). National Bureau of Economic Research.

US Equal Employment Opportunity Commission. 2017. "Sexual Harassment." https://www.eeoc.gov/laws/types/sexual_harassment.cfm.

Wakabayashi, D., and S. Shane. 2017. "Twitter, with Accounts Linked to Russia, to Face Congress over Role in Election." *New York Times* online, September 27. https://www.nytimes.com/2017/09/27/technology/twitter -russia-election.html.

Warshak, R. A. 2015. "Poisoning Parent-Child Relationships Through the Manipulation of Names." *American Journal of Family Therapy* 43, no. 1: 4–15.

"In 355 Days, President Trump Has Made 2,001 False or Misleading Claims." 2018. *Washington Post*, January 9. Accessed January 16, 2018. https://www.washingtonpost.com/graphics/politics/trump-claims-database/?tid=a_mcntx&utm_term=.9ed699034256.

Williams, A. 2017. "Have Your Representatives in Congress Received Donations from the NRA?" *Washington Post* online, October 5. https://www.washingtonpost.com/graphics/national/nra-donations/?utm_term=.5dcce8688a7d.

Wuest, J., and M. Merritt-Gray. 2016. "Beyond Survival: Reclaiming Self After Leaving an Abusive Male Partner." *Canadian Journal of Nursing Research Archive* 32 (4).

Yagoda, B. 2017. "How Old Is 'Gaslighting'?" *Chronicle of Higher Education*, January 12. Accessed January 12, 2018. https://www.chronicle.com/blogs/linguafranca/2017/01/12/how-old-is-gaslight/.

INDEX

ABOUT THE AUTHOR

Stephanie Moulton Sarkis PhD is a bestselling author and therapist specializing in gaslighting. She is a Diplomate and Clinical Mental Health Specialist in Child and Adolescent Counseling with the American Mental Health Counselors Association. She is also a National Certified Counselor, Licensed Mental Health Counselor, and a Florida Supreme Court Certified Family and Circuit Mediator. Dr. Sarkis is the founder of the Sarkis Institute, and is a blogger for *Psychology Today* and *The Huffington Post*. She has a PhD, EdS, and MEd in Mental Health Counseling from the University of Florida. She is also an expert in attention deficit hyperactivity disorder, chronic pain, and anxiety disorders. She is in private practice in Tampa, Florida. You can visit her website at www.stephaniesarkis.com.